the total
gym ball workout

Note
Whilst every effort has been made to ensure that the content of this book is as technically accurate and as sound as possible, neither the author nor the publishers can accept responsibility for any injury or loss sustained as a result of the use of this material.

Published by Bloomsbury Publishing Plc
49–51 Bedford Square, London WC1B 3DP
www.bloomsbury.com

First edition 2011

ISBN 9781 4081 4199 1

A CIP catalogue record for this book is available from the British Library.

Acknowledgements
Cover photographs © Grant Pritchard
Inside photographs pp 6, 9, 11, 14, 18, 21, 24, 26, 40, 43, 45, 99 © Shutterstock; pp 1, 5, 13, 31, 41, 106 courtesy and © Copyright of Escape Fitness Ltd
Illustrations by David Gardner
Designed by James Watson
Commissioned by Charlotte Croft
Edited by Kate Wanwimolruk

This book is produced using paper that is made from wood grown in managed, sustainable forests. It is natural, renewable and recyclable. The logging and manufacturing processes conform to the environmental regulations of the country of origin.

Typeset in 10.25pt on 13.5pt URWGroteskLig by Margaret Brain, Wisbech

Printed and bound in China by C & C Offset Printing

the total
gym ball workout

TRADE SECRETS OF A PERSONAL TRAINER

STEVE BARRETT

BLOOMSBURY

disclaimer and advisory

Before attempting any form of exercise, especially that which involves lifting weights, always ensure you have a safe working environment. Ensure that the floor surface you are on is non-slip and do not stand on any rugs or mats that could move when you exercise. Also, clear your exercise space of items that could cause you harm if you collided with them; this includes furniture, pets and children. Pay particular attention to the amount of clearance you have above your head and remember that for some of the exercise moves you will be raising your hands and the weights above head height, so keep away from doorways and light fittings.

The information, workouts, health related information and activities described in this publication are practiced and developed by the author and should be used as an adjunct to your understanding of health and fitness and, in particular, strength training. While physical exercise is widely acknowledged as being beneficial to a participant's health and well-being, the activities and methods outlined in this book may not be appropriate for everyone. It is fitness industry procedure to recommend all individuals, especially those suffering from disease or illness, to consult their doctor for advice on their suitability to follow specific types of activity. This advice also applies to any person who has experienced soft tissue or skeletal injuries in the past, those who have recently received any type of medical treatment or are taking medication and women who are, or think they may be, pregnant.

The author has personally researched and tried all of the exercises, methods and advice given in this book, on himself and with many training clients. However, this does not mean these activities are universally appropriate and neither he nor the publishers are, therefore, liable or responsible for any injury, distress or harm that you consider may have resulted from following the information contained in this publication.

contents

1 the basics of exercising with a gym ball

the S.A.F.E. trainer system
(Simple, Achievable, Functional, Exercise)

. . . .

We need to exercise our bodies in a way that is achievable, effective and, most of all, sustainable so that the method becomes part of our lifestyle, rather than an inconvenience.

In a perfect world everyone would be able to lift their own body weight above their head, have ideal body fat levels and be able to run a four-minute mile. Any one of these goals is achievable if you are highly motivated and have very few other commitments in your life, but the reality is that most people are so far off this state of perfection that the biggest challenge is either starting an exercise programme, or staying committed and engaged with a method of training for long enough to see any kind of improvement.

Exercise is in many ways a perfect product, because it has very few negative side effects, it is cheap to do and highly versatile. But so many high profile, quick-fix programmes and products make exercise sound easy, as though it is a magic wand that once waved will bring near instant results. And with the fitness industry constantly driven by innovation in products and methods, the diverse and sometimes bewildering amount of advice available makes it all too easy to be overwhelmed. The truth is that many training programmes and methods will theoretically work, but the level of commitment needed is so high that when you add in work and family responsibilities, stress and other demands upon time, most of us simply cannot stick to a plan.

I also find that those programmes which seem too good to be true usually have a series of components that are not explicit in the headline, but are required to achieve the spectacular results it boasts about. So you sign up to a workout programme claiming: 'Instant fat loss – ultra 60 second workout!' only to find that to achieve the promised weight loss you have to go on an impossible 500 calorie a day diet. These methods also assume that everybody is fairly perfect already; by this I mean they don't have any injuries, they are strong, mobile and flexible and have a cardiovascular system that will soak up anaerobic training from day one. If these people are out there I don't see them walking up and down the average high street. There is a real need to approach fitness in a more down to earth, less sensationalist way. We need to exercise our bodies in a way that is achievable, effective and, most of all, sustainable so that the method becomes part of our lifestyle, rather than an inconvenience.

My S.A.F.E. trainer system (Simple, Achievable, Functional, Exercise) is all of these things. It is based on 20 years of personal training experience, including many thousands of hours of coaching, lifting, running, jumping and stretching with people from all walks of life, from the average man or woman to elite athletes. My system respects the natural way that the body adapts to activity and creates a perfect physiological learning curve.

All S.A.F.E. trainer system moves develop stability, strength or power. If you're not familiar with these essential components of human performance, I am sure that you will recognise the saying: 'You have to walk before you can run'. This is the epitome of my approach, because when a client says they want to run or jump, the first thing I have to establish as a personal trainer is that they are at least already at the walking stage. I consider stability to be the walking phase of human movement, as it teaches you the correct muscle recruitment patterns; strength the running phase, as it trains the body to do these moves against a greater force (resistance); and power the jumping phase, since it teaches you to add speed and dynamics to the movement.

Like many of the most popular pieces of fitness equipment the gym ball was originally developed for use as a rehabilitation tool and then progressively became popular as a fitness product. Many of the exercises performed on the ball were originally conceived to strengthen individuals returning to exercise from an injury – when the gym balls crossed over from being a rehab tool to becoming one of the most popular items of fitness equipment those exercises became increasingly incorporated into fitness programmes which is entirely logical when you consider that for many fitness professionals their first experience of using a gym ball was when they required treatment for an injury. This book focuses on all the positive reasons for using a ball and aims to help you enhance the results you get from the time you spend doing strength and conditioning training and will hopefully encourage you to think of a gym ball as something that is more than simply a comfortable place to do sit ups. When you get to the portfolio of exercises (see page 43) demonstrating the actual exercises (or 'moves' as I like to call them) you will find that, rather than just being a list of exercises with a gym ball, I have focused on the moves that really work. There are hundreds of moves that can be done with a ball, but many of them are very similar to each other, ineffective or potentially dangerous. This book is all about combining skills and methods to create safe and effective fitness ideas to help you get the most out of your time with the ball.

You'll find that the majority of the exercises progress through three stages; I don't like to refer to these as easy, medium and advanced because in reality some of the changes are very subtle while on others you would really notice if you were to try all three versions back to back. Instead, the following three levels closely mirror the systematic approach athletes use in the weight training room and on the training field:

1 Each move can be progressed or regressed by changing body position.
2 Resistance is applied to the move.
3 The speed at which the move is performed is increased (or in fact a combination of all three).

Remember, if you're moving you're improving.

how to use this book

To help you make sense of each gym ball activity and how it relates to my S.A.F.E. training system, each move is classified by its respective outcome, whether that be an increase in stability, strength or power, rather than the less subjective easy, medium and hard.

Training with a gym ball is not only safe but is also a very efficient use of your time. Clearly, the amount of time you spend on the ball will dictate the outcomes, however, of all the pieces of fitness equipment available, the gym ball more than any other will give greater results if you also aim for quality rather than sheer quantity. The gym ball has in a very short time become an indispensable tool, not just for the world of health and fitness, but also for sportsmen and women. The possibilities are endless, and no matter whether your goals are strength, mobility, balance, co-ordination or simply a desire for cosmetically firmer more toned muscles, a gym ball can play a significant part in helping you to achieve them.

When I started to think about writing this book, the first thing I had to come to terms with is that there are many other books available that set out to teach you how to use a gym ball. Likewise, in my everyday life as a personal trainer I know that my clients have access to information not only from myself, but from a wide range of sources such as the web, books and no doubt other personal trainers they come across in the gym.

As I have worked with many of my clients now for over a decade, clearly they find my approach productive and a worthwhile investment. With this in mind, my aim is to condense 25 years' experience of training my own body and, more importantly, 20 years' experience as a personal trainer and many thousands of hours of training the bodies of other people into this book.

Don't worry: this isn't an autobiography in which I wax lyrical about the celebrities and Premier League footballers I've trained. Yes, I have trained those types of people, but to me every client has the same goal for every training session: they want to get maximum results from the time they are prepared to invest in exercise. Every exercise I select for their session, therefore, has to have earned its place in the programme and every teaching point that I provide needs to be worthwhile and have a positive outcome. In essence, my teaching style could almost be described as minimalist. Now that the fitness industry enters its fourth decade, many of you will have accumulated a level of knowledge and information equal to some fitness professionals in the industry, so I don't go in for trying to show you how clever I am when all that is required are clear and concise instructions.

I learned this lesson many years ago when I was hired as personal trainer to a professor of medicine. There was absolutely nothing I could say about the function of the body that she didn't already know, but what I could do was assess her current level of ability and take her on the shortest, safest and most effective route to an improved level of fitness. Fifteen years on I am still finding new ways to help her enjoy and benefit from the time we spend training together.

The thought process and methods I use are based on my belief that everybody feels better when they build activity into their lives, but not everybody has the motivation and time to create the type of bodies we see on the covers of fitness magazines. When training my clients, I am ultimately judged on the results I deliver. These results can present themselves in many ways, for example, in the mirror or on the weighing scales, but I also aim to help my clients make sense of what we are doing together. I find when talking about any activity it is best to focus on the outcomes rather than use subjective classifications, such as beginner/advanced, easy/hard. Therefore, to help you make sense of each activity you'll be doing on the gym ball, and how it relates to my S.A.F.E. training system, each move is classified by its respective outcome, whether that be an increase in stability, strength or power, rather than the less subjective easy, medium and hard.

every body is different

Just to be clear, any attempt to classify physical activity has to respect the fact that each human body responds to physical demands differently – there isn't an exact point where one moves stops being beneficial for stability and switches over to being purely for strength. The transition is far more subtle and means that no matter which version of a move you are doing, you will never be wasting your time.

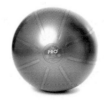

don't skip the moves

Human nature might lead you to think that the way to achieve the quickest results would be to skip the stability and strength moves and start on day one with the power versions. Overcoming this instinct is the fundamental difference between the 'old school approach' of beating up the body every training session, rather than using your training time wisely. My approach is about quality and not quantity. For a personal trainer to take this approach it requires true confidence and belief in the system, as some clients (particularly men) feel that they should be 'working hard' every session. This I feel is a situation unique to fitness training. In no other sport or activity would you set out to teach the body to cope with a new skill or level of intensity by starting with the high intensity or fastest version. For example, if you are learning to play golf, you don't start by trying to hit the ball a long way, rather you start by simply trying to make contact and hit it in the right direction. Or how about tennis? When learning to serve, if all you do is hit the ball as hard as you can, it is unlikely that any shot will ever stay within the lines of the court and therefore count. In all cases quality and the development of skill is the key to success.

mixing it up

The invention of the gym ball triggered a need for personal trainers to think about human movement in a completely new way, so personal trainers, coaches and instructors now think very differently about exercise today compared to just ten years ago – this new mindset and way of thinking is responsible for the proliferation of the word 'functional' being used to be used to describe exercise that has a direct relationship with the way we move in every day life or during sporting activities. In just one decade the trend has gone from doing much of our

strength training on machines that moved in straight lines to trying to incorporate the body's three planes of motion (sagittal, transverse and frontal) into all our conditioning exercises by using both improved weight machines, and of course the huge selection of functional training products now available: sagittal involves movements from left to right of the body's centre line; frontal (coronal) involves movements which are forward and backward from the centre line and transverse which are movements that involve rotation. The reality is these planes of motion never occur independently of each other so actually the best way to ensure you are working through all three planes is to create exercises that incorporate bending and twisting rather than look at joint movements in isolation.

Before the fitness industry started to think with a 'functional' mindset it wasn't unusual to discourage any type of twisting during a workout; the introduction of functional training equipment and in particular the gym ball has evoked a completely different approach where we now actively look for ways to incorporate all the planes of motion into everything we do. The multi-plane moves don't altogether replace isolation moves that still have an important role to play (particularly if you are trying to overload and bulk up individual muscles). These isolation moves are generally good for overloading and challenging an individual muscle to adapt and react to the challenges of exercise, but working muscles one at a time leaves you with a body full of great individual muscle when what you actually need are muscles that work as a team and in conjunction with other muscles that surround them. For example, despite most of the classic free weight exercises being integrated movements (i.e. they work more than one set of muscles at a time), the vast majority of free weight moves involve no rotation of the spine (through the transverse plane) and therefore don't train the body for the reality of everyday where we constantly rotate at the same time as bending, pushing or pulling against external forces, but working muscles one at a time is not what a gym ball session sets out to do. Even when the moves are highly targeted at smaller muscle groups, such as the pecs and the triceps, being on the ball enables them to be 'functional' rather than isolated, because in addition to the muscles being intentionally targeted, they have the additional benefit of directing force through the spine and lumbopelvic region and therefore activate the core stabilisers in a way that wouldn't occur if the same muscles were worked off the ball.

I can honestly say that until the late 1990s not a second thought was given to the muscles that we now refer to as 'core stabilisers'. As with many new items of equipment, for a short time the gym ball was all-encompassing and there was a trend to do absolutely everything we had previously done on a bench or on the floor on the ball. For many moves that was fine, but it didn't work for the isolation moves targeting smaller muscle groups like biceps – simply doing bicep curls sat on the ball added nothing to the activity, in fact, doing the bicep curl standing up is likely to stimulate more muscle activity because the legs are fully load bearing. With this in mind, when working with a gym ball we rarely incorporate isolation moves as this defeats the object of being on the ball in the first place.

When using a gym ball for fitness, rather than rehabilitation, it is important not to become obsessed with doing everything on the ball and to try to incorporate other types of activity into your week. Many of the moves that follow in this book are to be performed in the prone position (lying face up), so while they are highly productive, it is wise to make them a part of your active lifestyle rather than relying on them to be your single dominant form of exercise. Therefore, I suggest that every session you spend on the ball you should also try to build in time for upright free-flowing activity, such as walking, jogging or running.

the workouts

In the final section of the book you will find a series of workouts. They are designed to be realistic sessions that you can do on any day of the week, without the need for 'rest' days or anything more than a reasonable amount of space.

All the workouts are sequential, so in theory you could start with 15 minutes of stability moves and do every workout until you reach 45 minutes of power moves. This is, of course, the theory; in reality you will naturally find the right start point depending on how you do with the assessment (see page 'Assess, don't guess' on page 25) and how much time you have available on a given day. Continue using that particular workout until you feel ready to move on. I would advise everybody to start with the stability sessions, then move onto strength and then finally power, but I also accept that some people will find that the stability and strength moves don't challenge them enough so they will dive into the power phase. Please bear in mind that, if this is how you plan on approaching the exercises in this book, you might be missing out on a valuable learning curve that the body would benefit from.

a resource for life

My aim is for this book to be an ongoing reference point, and I suggest reading the entire contents and then dipping into the specific areas that interest you, such as the training programmes or fitness glossary. I guarantee you'll discover nuggets of information that perhaps you knew a little about, but had never fully understood because they had been explained in such a way that left you confused. If fitness training is an important part of your life, or even your career, then I know this book will be a long-term resource and will help you get the most from the time you spend using gym balls.

FAQs

When learning to train with a gym ball, there are a handful of important questions that you should ask before starting. Find the answers here.

These are the most common questions that fitness trainers are asked in relation to exercising with a gym ball.

Does using a gym ball create better results and, if so, why?

Yes, but like all fitness equipment it will only help you to get better results if you use it to enhance the individual exercise, rather than for the sake of it. Simply sitting on the ball won't transform an exercise into something special – the purpose of the ball is to add to the physical challenge of performing that movement. Very simply, a sit-up on the floor recruits the muscles required to help you sit up, whereas a sit-up on the gym ball recruits the same muscles as the floor version, as well as those muscles that stop you from rolling off the ball. The only time I use a gym ball is when doing so will make the exercise more productive, for example, doing bicep curls while sitting on a gym ball won't have some additional magical effect on your fitness, so I would rather do bicep curls standing up.

The reason for doing anything on a ball is that the ball creates an 'environment' or reaction in the body that adds to the exercise by increasing muscle action, the amount of muscles actively recruited and exertion levels.

How does a gym ball add to an individual exercise or entire workout?

There are two main reasons for using a gym ball in your workout. First, because of the very flexible tactile surface, you can use a ball to get into advantageous positions that you couldn't achieve without it. Most of these positions 'trick' the body to work productively against its own weight or external resistance, such as if you're holding dumbbells. For example, when we perform a dumbbell chest press on a solid bench the bench provides a stable surface to push against and therefore those muscles not involved in moving the weights up and down are fairly redundant. However, when you perform a dumbbell chest press on a gym ball, in addition to the muscles of the chest and arms working to move the weight every other major muscle will be active to hold your body in position on the ball.

Second, due to the unstable nature of the ball, the body generates involuntary muscle actions/activity which allows you to target muscles that would ordinarily be less involved if the same move was performed on a solid surface. This additional muscle activity is generated by both the visible/touchable surface muscles and those deep internal muscles within the cavity of the torso that are classified as core stabilisers; the pelvic floor is a great example of a set of muscles that play hardly any role in a floor-based sit-up, but when performed on a gym ball they spring into action to work in conjunction with the large external muscles, such as the gluteus maximus.

So we can use a gym ball to train the core, but that seems to apply to so many types of exercise. What is the core, and why is using a gym ball such a good way to target it?

One of the most abused statements in the world of fitness must be: 'this exercise will work your core', perhaps because such a claim increases the kudos of the activity in the mind of the participant. However, in the case of exercising with gym balls it is actually true. This form of exercise has its origins in rehabilitation and became increasingly popular at the same time global populations were becoming less active, increasingly obese and more prone to injuries, aches and pains that could often be traced back to a lack of activity, rather than the wrong activity.

what is 'core training'?

This subject can get very confusing so I thought it might help if I gave you my one line description of what I think core training is.

Core training is: 'Exercise that develops strength and endurance for all muscles that protect the spine from damage and that function to produce dynamic movements'.

Or, the even shorter version: 'Exercise that makes you better at dealing with forces applied to the lumbopelvic region'.

As core training has evolved from physical therapy, where the main aim is to fix problems rather than achieve traditional fitness or cosmetic outcomes, there is a tendency to medicalise the use of gym balls. However, since my aim is to increase fitness rather than to use the ball for therapy, I approach core training with the same attitude as I do all of my training: you need to walk before you can run. Therefore, if I find that a person is having issues with their balance, stability and overall quality of movement, then I absolutely start from the beginning using the ball to re-train them to use (help activate) muscles and maintain postures at the lowest of intensity before moving on to what they would consider to be a 'workout'. But unlike many personal trainers who seem to revel in finding things wrong with their clients, I do not believe that everybody in some way is bound to be broken if they have not previously done 'core training'. Therefore, if you are healthy and injury free working the core does not need to feel like a visit to the doctor; it can and should be challenging and progressive but, above all, simple.

the core muscles

The lumbopelvic region consists of the deep torso muscles, transversus abdominis, multifidus, internal obliques and the layers of muscle and fascia that make up the pelvic floor. These are key to the active support of the lumbar spine, but unfortunately they are also the most vulnerable to injury if neglected. Using a gym ball as a semi-stable platform to support the body when doing strength and conditioning exercises recruits these muscles and is particularly productive because the muscle activity is involuntary so, rather than having to tell the body to do something, it simply gets on with the work that is required. In fact, these muscles are recruited a split second before any movements of the limbs, which suggests that the muscle actually anticipates the force that will soon be going through the lumber spine.

There are hundreds of moves that you can do on a gym ball, especially with dumbbells, so why not just do everything on a ball?

There are hundreds of moves, but that doesn't mean they are productive. There is a misconception that doing exercise you would normally perform standing up is in some way improved if you perform it while sitting on a gym ball, such as a shoulder press, lateral raise or front raise with dumbbells. But, actually, each of these moves produces greater functional benefits when performed in a standing position because human beings have been standing on two feet for thousands of years. Therefore, if you want to incorporate the challenge of stability products into standing exercises, rather than sit down on a ball, I suggest using products such as wobble boards, the BOSU® (Both sides up) and the Reebok Core Board®.

Does sitting on a gym ball while at my desk give my core muscles a workout?

This depends upon what you class as a workout. The honest answer is that merely sitting on a gym ball isn't going to prompt the deep core muscles to do anything dramatic. However, I encourage anybody whose life revolves around 'the three Cs' (those who go from chair, to car, to computer and back again). For these 'professional sitters', sitting on a gym ball rather than a chair will at least make them more aware of their posture during the desk-bound parts of their day, as it is frankly difficult to slouch on a gym ball.

What size ball do I need?

This depends upon what you predominately intend to do with your ball. Gym balls from the top manufacturers have a standardised sizing system and your selection should be based on your height.

Table 1 Gym ball sizing system	
User height (cm)	**Ball size (cm)**
160–175	Small (55)
176–195	Medium (65)
196+	Large (75)

If you intend to use the gym ball purely for sitting, then go one size smaller than the usual recommendations, as this will be most comfortable.

How hard should a gym ball be blown up?

An under- or over-inflated ball will not perform correctly. If a ball is too soft you will just sink into the surface and if a ball is over-inflated it will cause the user to balance on top of it, rather than allowing the ball to mould to the user's body shape.

When you inflate a gym ball you ideally should inflate it to approximately 80 per cent of its total inflation, then leave it for 24 hours to allow the material to settle, then finish the inflation process. Rather than try to measure air pressure inside the ball, measure the diameter: place the ball right up against a wall, hold a straight edge against the point on the ball that is furthest from the wall (the edge needs to extend to the floor), then measure the distance along the floor from the wall to this point.

Why do the prices of gym balls vary so much?

The cost of a ball reflects its ability to perform and the quality of the materials used to make it. A cheap ball might be cheap for many reasons, but it is mainly due to the thickness and cost of the raw materials combined with mass-production manufacturing methods. More expensive balls are generally thicker, have more raw materials and take longer to manufacture. They can be inflated with greater amounts of pressure without becoming 'thin' (think about it – if you keep blowing a balloon up, it gets thinner and thinner right up to the point it pops). The best quality balls have a higher level of tolerance against both static and dynamic forces, which are the figures you need to take in to account when deciding if a gym ball is strong enough for your needs (you can usually find this information printed on the ball or its packaging).

What does 'anti-burst' mean – are gym balls indestructible?

No, a gym ball is not indestructible. Anti-burst means that if the balls fails, it will deflate gradually rather than pop like a balloon. Gym balls – in particular those intended for professional use – always come with very specific warranty restrictions because, while they can withstand massive forces, they can sustain invisible damage if kicked or used inappropriately.

Can I use a gym ball outdoors?

Only if it used on some kind of mat that completely protects it from any sharp or rough surfaces. Personally I would not risk it.

Is it safe to use free weights on a gym ball?

Yes, as long as the gym ball you are using has both dynamic and static capabilities of withstanding the weight of the free weights and the person combined.

I see people standing on gym balls in the gym – what does that achieve?

I ask myself the same question all the time. Again, people believe that this works the core, but the only 'benefit' I can think of for putting yourself in that position is that you'll get really good at standing on a gym ball, rather than developing universal skills that will be beneficial in your daily life.

find your starting point

Before starting any exercise programme, test your body against the fitness checklist: mobility, flexibility, muscle recruitment and strength.

Before you think about getting on a gym ball you need to establish what your starting point is, i.e. your current level of fitness, mobility, flexibility and strength any consideration. Every first consultation with a new personal training client revolves around the wish list of goals they hope to achieve. This list inevitably combines realistic goals with entirely unrealistic aims. Invariably people focus on their 'wants' rather than their 'needs' when goal setting, and there is a big difference between the two mindsets. While 'wanting' could be considered a positive attitude, it will never overcome the need to slowly expose the body to processes that will change its characteristics and ability. Men in particular want to dive in at the most advanced stage of training, but it makes no sense to overload a muscle if your quality of movement is lacking.

realistic goal setting

Want (v) 'A desired outcome'
Need (n) 'Circumstances requiring some course of action'

By identifying your needs, your goals may not sound so spectacular but you are more likely to achieve better and longer term results, and your progress through the fitness process will be considerably more productive. Therefore, rather than thinking about the ultimate outcome, think instead of resolutions to the 'issues'.

fitness checklist

The checklist you need to put your body through before you start rolling around on a gym ball is very simple and logical. Our ability to lift/move weight (by which I mean body weight as well as external loads) relies on a combination of:

- Mobility
- Flexibility
- Muscle recruitment
- Strength

· ·

If any of these vital components is neglected, it will have a knock-on effect on your progress. For example, while you may have the raw strength in your quadriceps to squat with a heavy weight, if you do not have a full range of motion in the ankle joints and sufficient flexibility in the calf muscles, then your squat will inevitably be of poor quality. Likewise, in gyms it is common to see men who have overtrained their chest muscles to such an extent that they can no longer achieve scapular retraction (they are round shouldered and therefore demonstrate poor technique in moves that require them to raise their arms above their heads).

This type of checklist is traditionally the most overlooked component of strength training and, while testing weight, body fat levels and cardiac performance is now a regular occurrence in the fitness industry, the introduction of screening for quality of movement has taken a much longer time to become a priority. This, despite a self-administered assessment can be as simple as looking in the mirror.

assess, don't guess

There is no better summary of how important our ability to move freely is than in one of my favourite sayings: 'Use it or lose it'. This says it all – if you don't use the body to perform physical tasks it will more likely deteriorate rather than just stay the same.

It maybe no coincidence that assessing movement quality has grown in importance today for athletes and fitness enthusiasts at the same pace as the popularity of functional training – rightly so because if you don't assess yourself then how can you know what areas of functionality you need to work on most? Before functional training became a key component of progressive fitness programmes all the progressions related to increasing duration and intensity and resistance, however now the quality of movement has become of equal importance.

Today, the assessment of 'functional movement', or biomechanical screening, is its own specialised industry within the world of fitness. Those working in orthopaedics and conventional medical rehabilitation have always followed some form of standardised assessment where they test the function of the nerves, muscles and bones before forming an opinion of a patient's condition. Becoming a trained practitioner takes many years of study and practice. Not only must a practitioner gain knowledge of a wide spectrum of potential conditions, but just as importantly they must understand when and how to treat their patient, or when they need to refer them to other colleagues in the medical profession. Having been subjected to and taught many different approaches to movement screening, in my mind, the challenge isn't establishing there is something 'wrong', rather it is knowing what to do to rectify the issue.

mobility and flexibility

The most common problem limiting quality of movement in the average person is a lack of mobility and flexibility, which can be provisionally tested using the standing twist and the overhead squat assessment (see below).

To understand why mobility is key to human movement, think how as babies we start to move independently. We are born with mobility and flexibility, then we progressively develop stability, balance and then increasing amounts of strength. As we get older we may experience injuries, periods of inactivity and, to some extent, stress which all contribute towards a progressive reduction of mobility. There is no better summary of how important mobility is than in one of my favourite sayings: 'Use it or lose it'. If you sit for extended periods or fail to move through the three planes of motion (see page 151), then you invariably become restricted in your motion. With this in mind, I hope you can see that lifting weights without first addressing mobility issues is like trying to build the walls of a house before you have completed the foundations.

The following two mobility tests challenge the entire length of the kinetic chain (actions and reaction to force that occur throughout the bones, muscles and nerves whenever dynamic motion or force is required from the body) and help to reveal if you are ready to move beyond bodyweight moves to begin adding the additional loads such as dumbbells. This test focuses on the following key areas of the shoulders, the mid-thoracic spine, the pelvis, the knees, ankles and feet. Any limitation of mobility, flexibility or strength in these areas will show up as either an inability to move smoothly through the exercise or an inability to hold the body in the desired position.

Test 1 standing twist

This is the less dramatic of the two mobility tests and serves to highlight if you have any pain that only presents when you move through the outer regions of your range of movement, and also if you have a similar range of motion between rotations on the left and right sides of your body.

- Stand with your feet beneath your hips.
- Raise your arms to chest height then rotate as far as you can to the right, noting how far you can twist.
- Repeat the movement to the left.
- Perform the movement slowly so that no 'extra twist' is achieved using speed and momentum.

Your observation is trying to identify any pain and/or restriction of movement. If you find either, it might be the case that this reduces after a warm-up or a few additional repetitions of this particular movement. If you continue to experience pain, you should consider having it assessed by a physiotherapist or sports therapist.

Test 2 overhead squat (OHS)

I've used the OHS test over 5000 times as part of my S.A.F.E. approach to exercise and I have found it to be the quickest and easiest way of looking at basic joint and muscle function without getting drawn in to speculative diagnosis of what is and isn't working properly. If you can perform this move without any pain or restriction, then you will find most of the moves in this book achievable. There is no pass or fail, rather you will fall into one of two categories: 'good' or 'could do better'. If you cannot achieve any of the key requirements of the OHS move, then it is your body's way of flagging up that you are tight and/or weak in that particular area. This, in turn, could mean you have an imbalance, pain or an untreated injury, which may not prevent you from exercising, but you should probably get checked out by a physiotherapist or sports therapist.

Perform this exercise barefoot and in front of a full-length mirror so that you can gain maximum information from the observation of your whole body. Also refer to table 1 for a list of key body regions to observe during this test. (This move also doubles up as a brilliant warm-up for many types of exercise including lifting weights.)

- Stand with feet pointing straight ahead and at hip width.
- Have your hands in the 'thumbs-up position' and raise your arms above your head, keeping them straight, into the top of a 'Y' position (with your body being the bottom of the 'Y'). Your arms are in the correct position when they are back far enough to disappear from your peripheral vision.

● The squat down is slow and deep, so take a slow count of six to get down by bending your knees. The reason we go slow is so you do not allow gravity to take over and merely slump down. Also, by going slow you get a chance to see and feel how everything is moving through the six key areas.

The magic of this move is that you will be able to see and feel where your problem spots are and, even better, the test becomes the solution, as simply performing it regularly helps with your quality of movement. Stretch out any area that feels tight and aim to work any area that feels weak.

Table 2 Key body regions to observe in the overhead squat		
Body region	**Good position**	**Bad position**
Neck		
Shoulders		
Mid-thoracic spine		
Hips		

Knees		

Ankles and feet		

As you perform the OHS you are looking for control and symmetry throughout and certain key indicators that all is well:

- Neck: You keep good control over your head movements and are able to maintain the arm lift without pain in the neck.
- Shoulders: In the start position and throughout the move you are aiming to have both arms lifted above the head and retracted enough so that they are outside your peripheral vision (especially when you are in the deep part of the squat). In addition to observing the shoulders look up at your arms to the hands – throughout the OHS you should aim to have your thumbs pointing behind you.
- Mid-thoracic spine: There is no instruction to keep your back straight, so in this area of the body you are looking for 'flow' rather than clunking movements.
- Hips: Imagine a straight line drawn directly down the centre of your body. Around the hips you are looking to see if you shift your weight habitually to one side, rather than keeping it evenly spread between both sides.
- Knees: The most common observation is the knees touching during the OHS, suggesting a weakness in the glutes. Less common is the knees parting, showing weakness in the inner thigh. Good technique is when your knees move forwards as you bend the legs. Note that clicking and crunching noises don't always suggest a problem unless they are accompanied by pain.
- Ankles and feet: The most obvious issue is the heels lifting from the floor, suggesting short achilles and calf muscles. Less obvious are the flattening of the foot arches that cause the feet to roll inward (overpronation) or the foot rolling outward (underpronation). Ideally, the foot should be in a neutral position.

If when you do the OHS in front of the mirror you observe any of these signals with your kinetic chain (the actions and reaction to force that occur throughout the bones, muscles and nerves whenever dynamic motion or force is required from the body), it really isn't the end of the world, in fact, most people find that they are tight in some areas (if not all of them) when they first try this test. The absolutely fantastic news is that if you do spot any issues, performing the OHS as an exercise, rather than merely a test, will improve your movement pattern, joint range and muscle actions over time.

overhead squat: the results

My rule is that if you cannot perform a perfect OHS, with none of the key warning signs listed above, then you are not ready to perform the power moves in the exercise portfolio. So, use the OHS as a guide to whether your body is as ready as your mind is to start doing the toughest, most challenging, exercises. If you find by doing the OHS that your body is not ready, don't think of it as a setback, but rather as a blessing: you are following a training method that is in tune with how the body works rather than one that merely sets out to punish it.

isolation vs integration

While intensity can be great, when you isolate your muscles you do not get the highly beneficial activity created by the rest of the kinetic chain. I am certainly not saying isolation moves are not productive, but with the biggest obstacle to exercise being a lack of time, integration work is going to have an instant usable impact on the entire body.

All movements that we do in training or everyday life can be classified as either isolation or integration moves. The vast majority of isolation moves have been created/invented to work specific muscles on their own, with the primary intention of fatiguing that muscle by working it in isolation, usually moving only one joint of the skeleton. Integration, or compound, moves are less of an invention and more of an adaptation of movement patterns that we perform in everyday life. They are designed to work groups of muscles across multiple joints all at the same time.

In real life we never isolate. Even when only a few joints are moving there is a massive number of muscles bracing throughout the body to let the prime muscles do their job. As you go about an average day I doubt you give a second thought to how you are moving. If you take the time to watch the world go by for a few hours, you will notice that human motion consists of just a few combinations of movements that together create the millions of potential moves we (hopefully) achieve everyday. Everything, and I mean everything, we do boils down to the following key movements:

- Push
- Pull
- Twist
- Squat
- Lunge
- Bend
- Walk
- Run
- Jump

Figure 1 The nine basic human movement patterns: (a) push, (b) pull, (c) twist, (d) squat, (e) lunge, (f) bend, (g) walk, (h) run and (i) jump

All of these movements are integrated. I am certainly not the first person to make this observation, but it constantly amazes me how my industry manages to complicate exercise. With this observation in mind, I am not a huge fan of old fashioned machines that isolate small areas of muscle to work them apparently more intensely. While intensity can be great, when you isolate you do not get the highly beneficial activity created by the rest of the kinetic chain. I am certainly not saying isolation moves are not productive, but with the biggest obstacle to exercise being a lack of time, integration work is going to have an instant usable impact on the entire body.

We would rarely incorporate isolation moves into a workout with a gym ball as this defeats the object of being on a ball in the first place. Even when a move is highly targeted towards smaller muscle groups, such as the pecs and the triceps, it would still be considered to be an integration (compound) move because, by sitting on the ball force is being directed through the lumbopelvic region, which therefore also activates the core stabilisers. Subsequently, the majority of the moves in this book are integrated, designed to achieve maximum results in the most economical amount of time.

learn it, then work it

As we have discovered, you must walk before you can run in any exercise method, and the body works best if you learn the activity prior to engaging in exercise, so that you will positively soak up the benefits.

Resistance training (using either body weight or free weights, or both) is very natural with hardly any complex skills required to achieve results. However, that is not to say you cannot do it incorrectly. In fact, along with failed runners, re-building the confidence of people who have tried resistance training and then failed or injured themselves has featured frequently in my working life. Because of this, I use the phrase 'learn it, then work it' to encourage people to take time to 'imprint' good quality movement patterns upon their bodies.

how to 'learn it, then work it'

How do you know what 'good quality' moves look like? Simply put, the move should look smooth and controlled and should not create pain in your joints. Aim to perform the concentric and eccentric phases (the lift and lower phases) at the same speed – lift for two counts and lower for two counts. When power and speed becomes more of an objective for you, aim to lift for one count and lower for two counts.

You can perform moves at slower speeds, but that then moves away from how we move/function in day to day life, rarely do we do any movement in slow motion just for the sake of it. It is really only beneficial to perform slow or super slow (quarter-speed) moves if you are training for specific sport activities, so as to prolong the time each muscle is under tension (known as 'time under tension'). Therefore, move at a natural speed: athletes and sports people train at 'real time' once they have learned the required movement pattern, so without even knowing it they are 'learning it, then working it'.

The beauty of grounding your workout in the 'learn it, then work it' approach is that by keeping the approach simple, achievable and functional you won't get tied up with methods that either do not work, or have ridiculous expectations of how much time you are going to dedicate to your fitness regime. As a personal trainer it can be hard to exercise in a gymnasium without wanting to question what many people are (think) they are doing. So often I see people doing difficult versions of exercises that are clearly beyond their level of ability — presumably because they think difficult/advance must equal quicker results. The obvious signs are that they can't control the weights or their body seems overpowered by the movements it is being asked to do — learn it, then work it relates to most physical tasks in life but especially sport, for example, if you has tennis lessons the first thing you would learn would be to make contact with the ball slowly rather than starting with the fastest hardest movements. So simply switch off your instincts to 'work hard' until you are satisfied that you can move and maintain quality and control throughout all the repetition.

As you get more adventurous and diverse with your exercise remember all your goals are achievable: remember, if you're moving you're improving.

'learn it, then work it' in sport

Practising movements in resistance training is paralleled in all performance-based sports. Athletes routinely perform low intensity 'drills', which echo the moves they need to make in their sport. For example, during almost every track session, sprinters practise knee lifts, heel flicks and other bounding exercises to improve their quality of movement and condition their muscles in a highly functional manner.

first you need stability

Stability is the first key ingredient to ensuring safe and effective exercise, the basic building block to everything that follows in this book.

To perform exercise safely and effectively, we have to firstly ensure our body is stable. The essence of stability is the ability to control and transfer force throughout the body. All human movement is, in fact, a chain of events involving the brain, the nervous system, muscles, fascia, ligaments and tendons. So, while a simple move like a bicep curl may appear to involve only activity from the shoulder down to the hand, in reality there is a chain of events that occur to ensure that the right amount of force is applied and that the two ends of the bicep are tethered to a stable base.

In essence, wherever there is visible movement in the body, there are always invisible reactions occurring within the kinetic chain to facilitate this movement.

The engine room of all this activity is in the deep muscles of the trunk and involves the:

- Transversus abdominus (TA)
- Multifidi (MF)
- Internal obliques
- Five layers of muscle and fascia that make up the pelvic floor.

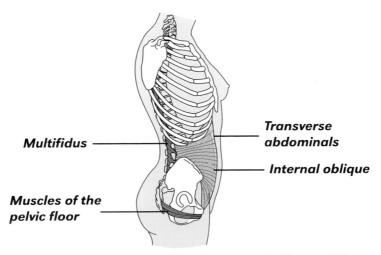

Multifidus

Transverse abdominals

Internal oblique

Muscles of the pelvic floor

Figure 2 The deep muscles of the trunk are crucial for stability

These muscles work as a team and their simultaneous contraction is known as 'co-contraction'. This complex muscle activity produces intra-abdominal pressure (IAP) and it is the creation of this pressure that stabilises the lumber spine. The misconception that the transversus abdominus looks like a 'belt' around the torso no doubt led fitness instructors to continuously advise clients to pull their stomach in (hollow the abdominal muscles), thinking that this would amplify the stability of the spine. However, it is not simply the recruitment of these muscles that instills strength and stability, but, more importantly, when they are recruited. In effect, they should have been advising clients to 'switch on' (brace their core).

remember: don't hollow your abs

Pulling in, or hollowing, the abs actually makes you less able to stabilise. If you imagine a tree that is perfectly vertical, but then you chop in or hollow out one side, the structure of the tree becomes less stable. I have two ways of coaching the correct technique to avoid hollowing the abs, depending on the client:

1 Switch on your abs as if you were going to get punched in the stomach, or
2 Engage the abs in the same way as if were about to be tickled.

Both methods achieve the desired outcome – with only a few of my male clients actually insisting that I really do hit them!

Stability is, therefore, a goal in everything that we do. However, we shouldn't have to undertake yet more training just to achieve core stability, rather we should ensure that the everyday movements we make encourage the muscles deep inside the trunk to work correctly during dynamic movements, and that the stabilisation is instinctive, as opposed to something that we have to remind ourselves to do every time. For instance, if you drop an egg in the kitchen and very quickly squat and make a grab to catch it, you don't stop to think: 'Did I line up my feet, pull my stomach in and keep my head up?' Actually, your body will have fired off a co-contraction which enabled you to grab the egg before it hit the ground (or, at least, make a good attempt). When I use this analogy to explain the concept of stability to my clients, they often get a twinkle in their eye, for if this process is instinctive, why should they continue to train? The reality, however, if that you still have to exercise that inclination to keep the system working properly: 'use it, or lose it'.

In the workout sessions later in this book, you will find that almost all the moves are classified as being good for stability. Since stability is the first stage of development, you might assume the strength and power moves that follow are more productive because they are more 'intense'. While this is true, that intensity will only be constructive if the body has the ability to control and direct all that extra force, which can only be learned through the stability moves.

the development of core stability in the fitness industry

During the 1990s, there were only three components of fitness that personal trainers focused on with the average client (by 'average' I mean a person looking for fitness gains rather than to compete in sport). Cardio was the route to cardiovascular efficiency and was the most obvious tool for weight loss; strength training isolated the larger muscle groups and gymnasiums were filled with straight line machines; and we only worked on flexibility because we knew we had to, but the chosen method was predominately the least productive type of stretching, i.e. static.

Then, it seems almost from nowhere, there was a new ingredient to every workout: core stability. New equipment such as Swiss balls and modern versions of wobble boards, such as the Reebok Core Board® and the BOSU® (Both sides up), increased the wave of enthusiasm for this type of training as, of course, did the new popularity for the more physical versions of yoga and Pilates.

In retrospect, we in the fitness industry could have thought to ourselves that we had been doing everything wrong up to that point. However, the reality is that rather than being 'wrong' we were just learning as we went along. In fact, many of the methods that suddenly became mainstream had been used in sports training for years before, but without the 'label' of core stability, and rather than treating them as an individual component, we trained them instinctively as part of our dynamic strength moves using body weight or free weights.

add some strength

The second key ingredient, there are several types of strength that you can gain performing these exercises with a gym ball.

When trying to establish a client's fitness objectives, 'I want to improve my strength' is often the only information given to a personal trainer. This seemingly simple request requires much more detail if you are going to achieve the outcome that is really desired.

The one-line definition of strength is: 'An ability to exert a physical force against resistance'. However, this catch-all is not specific enough when you are dealing with strength. In fact, there are three main types of strength:

1 Strength endurance: Achieved when you aim to exert force many times in close succession.
2 Elastic strength: Achieved when you make fast contractions to change position.
3 Maximum strength: Our ability over a single repetition to generate our greatest amount of force.

Each of these specific types of strength can be achieved using resistance either as individual components or preferably as part of an integrated approach.

Unless you are an athlete training for an event that requires a disproportionate amount of either endurance, elastic or maximum strength, then the integration of functional training methods will create a body that is more designed to cope with day to day life and amateur sports. While strength is an adaptation that the body willingly accepts, the reality is that changes take time, so treat strength gains as something that happens over weeks, months and years rather than mere days.

power and speed come with practice

The development of power in muscles is a rapid process and is also considerably practical, usable and functional for those men and women who have reached a point in their training where they have no need to be any 'stronger', but they want to make more of the strength they have.

Power is a measure of how much energy is created, the amount of force applied and the velocity at which it is applied. It is the ability to exert an explosive burst of movement. In everyday life it presents as bounding up stairs three at a time or pushing a heavy weight above your head. The development of power is not only a more rapid process than developing maximal strength, but is also considerably more practical, usable and functional for those men and women who have reached a point in their training where they have no desire to be any 'stronger', but they do want to make more of the strength they have. That is the point at which you stop thinking about increasing the amount of resistance you work against and start thinking about how to inject speed into the activity you are doing on the gym ball.

Let's make this simple. If you have two men of the same height, weight and with the same body fat levels and you challenge them to compete against each other in an explosive activity that they have both trained in, such as 20m sprint, then, apart from potential differences in reaction times, the man who wins that race will be the one who has a greater ability to utilise his strength and convert that strength into forward motion – this ability to use strength for explosive activity is power. The perfect exercise to generate this type of outcome would be the squat against wall with a jump as this move trains you to generate an explosive force that propels the body quickly.

When you get to the exercises in the portfolio classified as power moves you will see that they are in fact, progressions of the skills that you will have already developed during your stability and strength sessions, only performed at speed. In this respect, it becomes easier to understand why I advise not to skip a stage when learning movement patterns (learn it, then work it).

To train or develop power using predominately body weight exercises on a gym ball is realistic, but only as long as you do not get preoccupied with the speed part of the equation to the detriment of working against resistance. It is very easy to 'cheat' on a gym ball – cheating can be classed as not doing a full range of motion, shifting you body weight so that the exercise becomes easier or simply not putting any force against the contact points (your body on the ball and hands and feet) – any of these 'cheating tactics' will allow you to move faster but you will probably not be using as much strength as you would without the adaptation (cheat).

power and agility

Think of power as a very close relation of agility; you don't learn agility by overloading and working while fatigued, rather you develop it by achieving quality over quantity. In fact, introducing yourself to the pursuit of power can mean performing the moves without any weights and simply performing the movements fast with just body weight as the resistance, why? Because athletic power is actually a finely tuned combination of speed and strength.

2 the portfolio of moves

which moves should I do?

This section contains a portfolio of moves that I have selected from those I use every day with my personal training clients and are based on the principles I explained in the first part of this book. The only moves that have made it into this book are those that deserve to be here – every one of these moves is tried and tested to ensure it gets results, in fact, I have spent hundreds of hours using them myself and thousands of hours teaching them to my personal training clients, who over the years have included men and women from 16 to 86 years old, from size zero through to 280lbs. These clients have, justifiably, only been interested in the moves that work – and that is what you have here in this portfolio.

It is not an exhaustive list of moves, simply because many extra moves that could have been included use the gym ball simply as a 'prop' rather than a tool, or they are really just subtle adaptations of those included here. For instance, changes to foot position and the amount of bend that you have in your arms and legs will encourage the body to recruit slightly different muscles, but I would class these as adaptations rather than unique moves.

presentation of the moves

I wanted to show the moves as a complete portfolio, rather than simply wrapping them up into workouts, because you are then able to see how the stability, strength and power versions relate to each other. Understanding these progressions is something I encourage of my clients because they need to know that subtle changes can make all the difference between a good use of time and a waste of it. By thinking this way you can very quickly learn all the moves because, in the majority of cases, the main movement pattern stays the same throughout the stability, strength and power progressions, with only a slight change to the length of levers (arm/foot positions), range of motion or the speed.

dangerous gym ball moves

There will always be those people who dream up moves with a gym ball that are either dangerous, pointless or just plain stupid. The gym ball seems to attract these people more than any other item of equipment – I see people standing on balls, diving on balls, hitting balls and generally abusing themselves or the product. Just because you can do something on a ball, doesn't mean that it is productive or safe.

I also do not subscribe to the approach that if you perform a move on a gym ball it automatically becomes enhanced; it won't, for example, those people in the gym who spend their time sitting on a ball doing bicep curls need to stand up and get a move on. The only time my clients get to simply sit on the ball is if they have a ball at their desk instead of a chair.

The third part of this book then goes on to present a selection of training sessions, designed for a range of levels, and following my method of progressing through stability, strength and power exercises, no doubt some people will jump straight to the training sessions. However I find understanding the 'why' as well as knowing the 'how' generates better outcomes for most people so refer back to the portfolio of moves if you want the detailed description of how to perform the exercise. I have also provided you with a post-workout stretch session suitable for all types of resistance training (see pages 119–121). Please remember that you should always warm-up before embarking on any type of exercise.

every muscle plays a part

I purposefully haven't included diagrams of the muscles that are targeted by each move as hopefully by now you understand that, used correctly, every muscle plays a role in every move.

I have written the descriptions as if I am talking to you as a client – the key information for each explanation includes:

- the correct body position at the start and finish of the move;
- the movement that you are looking to create.

When I work with my PT clients I avoid over-coaching the movement as my goal is to see them move in a lovely 'fluid' way, where the whole movement blends together.

reps

This is a 'learn it' section rather than 'work it'. Therefore, for the vast majority of the moves I don't talk about how many repetitions you should do of each – that information is included in the workout section in the third part of the book. How many repetitions you perform should relate to your objectives; almost all the moves can be used to improve stability, strength and power (at the same time), and the speed and resistance at which you perform it will dictate the outcome. For example, a slow squat performed with a light weight will provide stability benefits. Exactly the same move performed with a heavier weight will increase strength and the same move at speed will develop power.

weight

As speed and resistance are both subjective (one person's 'light' is another person's 'heavy'), it is simply not possible predict how strong you are without seeing you actually work out, if you choose to use any of the moves that require dumbbells then choosing the correct weight is a matter of common sense, without being in the same room as you and looking at how you move and your physical characteristics to say exactly how much you should be lifting – my advice is always this, start with a weight that you can control but is challenging, as you fatigue lifting the weights gets harder and the last two repetitions of the set should be tough to do.

> ## tricks of the trade
> I have included a 'tricks of the trade' box which contains a nugget of information that I use to help my clients get the most out of each exercise.

key to exercises

As you move through the exercises, you will notice that each is identified by the following key words. A quick glance will tell you which element the move focuses on, what type of move it is and whether you need any additional equipment to perform it.

stability

Every move in this portfolio is a stability-enhancing exercise – yes, that includes the strength and power versions. Stability is, essentially, a reaction within the kinetic chain in which the body says to itself: 'Switch on the muscles around the lumbopelvic region, because this movement is looking for an anchor point to latch on to'. On this basis, you don't improve stability when you are sat down on a solid surface, but you do when sitting on a gym ball, neither do you generally improve it when a move involves just one joint.

strength

We could get all deep and meaningful about biomechanics here, but to qualify as a strength move, the exercise needs to be making you move a force through space using muscle contractions. Therefore anything that only involves momentum is a waste of time because you are just going along for the ride and not actively contracting your muscles. However, don't confuse speed with momentum – speed is good, especially when mixed with strength, because that combination develops the highly desirable power.

power

Every time you read the word 'power' you need to think of speed, and vice versa. The maths and physics required to understand how we measure power are enough to make you glaze over, and in reality you are much better off measuring your power ability by doing a simple time-trial sprint, or time yourself over a set number of repetitions, rather than trying to calculate exactly how much power you are exerting for a specific exercise.

If you want more power, you need to move fast, but you need to be able to maintain speed while pushing or pulling a weight (that weight could be an object or your own body). For example, you might have a guy who can skip across a shot put circle faster than the other guy when not holding and throwing the shot, but he is only speedy. The guy who can move fast and launch the shot (using strength) is the one with all the power.

the classic moves

exercise 1 sit-up arms at waist

● **stability**

a   b

- Start with your feet shoulder width apart and your hands at your waist. The ball should be between your pelvis and your shoulder blades.
- Lift your upper body from the ball, then lower under control.

> **tricks of the trade**
>
> Don't just rest the hands at your waist – actively press them against the hips and you will find the entire move feels stronger.

exercise 2 sit-up hands at head

• stability • strength

a   b

- Start with your feet shoulder width apart and your hands at your head so that the weight of the arms increases the challenge. The ball should be between your pelvis and your shoulder blades.
- Without 'throwing' your arms forward lift the upper body from the ball, then lower under control.

> ## ! tricks of the trade
> If you find that your neck aches, press your tongue into the roof of your mouth. This increases activity in the muscles of the neck and throat and causes your head to feel less heavy.

exercise 3 sit-up arms extended

• stability • strength • power

a   b

- Start with your feet shoulder width apart and your arms raised above your head (in the correct position they should be covering your ears). This shifts your centre of gravity to make the upper body feel heavier. The ball should be between your pelvis and your shoulder blades.
- Lift your upper body from the ball and lower under control, maintaining good arm length.

> **tricks of the trade**
>
> If this move feels like you are swinging your arms and cheating, place a towel between your knees and squeeze it. This will tidy up the move and help you to focus your strength.

exercise 4 sit-up rotation, feet apart

● stability

a   b

- Start with your feet shoulder width apart. The ball should be between your pelvis and your shoulder blades.
- Using the opposite leg as a target reach across your body at the same time as lifting the spine off the ball, i.e. when using your left arm, reach towards the right leg and you will feel the work in the right side of your body, and the reverse when using your right arm.
- There is a tendency to sit upright, but because of the leverage the top part of the movement is wasted, so go past the point where you can still feel tension in the muscle.

> **! tricks of the trade**
>
> Position yourself on top of the ball rather than leaning against it. You may not be able to curl as high but you will be putting more force through the muscles.

exercise 5 sit-up, rotation, feet together

• stability • strength

a   b

Here your narrow foot position increases the challenge – with the feet being closer together you need to accept that you won't be able to lift or rotate as much as you can on the wide foot version above.

- Start with your feet together. The ball should be between your pelvis and your shoulder blades.
- As you lift and rotate aim to take the hand down the inside of the opposite leg.
- As you lower back down make sure you let the shoulder release back down to the ball.

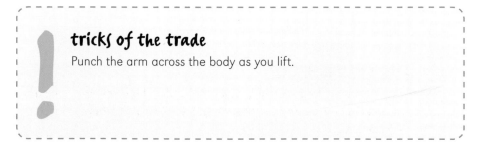

tricks of the trade
Punch the arm across the body as you lift.

exercise 6 sit-up reach, toe touch

• stability • strength • power

a   b

This move is performed quickly and therefore may look a little 'messy', which isn't really a problem and, in fact, if you keep it neat, the chances are that you are not really working fast enough.

The straighter you are able to keep the leg, the greater the resistance you are working against, so try to avoid simply sitting up, bending the knee and moving your foot towards the hand. It is much better to keep the leg long and to reach the foot by getting the upper body right up off the ball.

- Start with your feet shoulder width apart. The ball should be between your pelvis and your shoulder blades.
- Lift one leg and keep it extended straight out, you are going to reach for the foot with one hand.
- Your arm and leg start to move at the same time – it is hard, but try not to generate all the movement with your arm and leg: make sure some of the work is coming from the torso.

> **! tricks of the trade**
> Some of my personal training clients think they have failed on this if they don't touch their foot, but don't worry – it could be that you have really long legs!

exercise 7 seated pelvic tilt

● stability

a   b

This is one of the first moves a physiotherapist will do with patients to encourage them to generate more muscle activity in the lower abdominals. You need to sit tall on the ball (for some people even this is hard).

● Start with your feet hip width apart. You should be sitting tall on top of the ball rather than leaning against the side.
● Hold the start position for a couple of seconds, then roll your hips/pelvis underneath the body until the spine has gone from its extended start position to flexion. The best way of knowing that you have the move correct is that you will feel your bottom being rolled into the ball.
● This move is most productive when performed slowly so really prolong the movement as you work through the complete range of motion.

> **! tricks of the trade**
>
> OK, so you may feel rather silly doing this move in the gym. If you need to make it look more exciting, raise your arms in front of you and press the palms of your hands together. Personal trainers need to be experts at keeping their clients focused and this little trick keeps them tuned in and produces a contralateral contraction within the muscles of the chest, shoulders and arms.

exercise 8 sit-up knee raise, feet apart

• **stability** • **strength**

a  b

Timing is important in this move; you should aim to be lifting your leg at the same time as you lift your upper body. Try to make the movement smooth – avoid any 'punctuation' during the move.

- Start with your feet shoulder width apart. The ball should be between your pelvis and your shoulder blades.
- 'Throw' your arms forward to create a small amount of momentum, then reach between your legs towards your knees.
- You really know when you are doing this move well when you are able to push the supporting foot hard into the floor as you lift up.

> **!** **tricks of the trade**
> When I have a client with limited coordination I make them practice the rhythm of this move while standing up, which really helps.

exercise 9 sit-up knee raise, feet together

• stability • strength • power

a   b

Speed is essential to the success of this move. Finding a balance between the amount of leg lift and upper body lift is key, so aim to lift the leg to the same height as the chest.

- Start with your feet together. The ball should be between your pelvis and your shoulder blades.
- 'Throw' your arms forward to create a small amount of momentum, then keep your hands beside your head.
- While it is tempting, don't simply fall back onto the ball – lower yourself back down under control.

> ! **tricks of the trade**
>
> I find that pretending you are holding a ball in your hands and that you are 'throwing' the ball over your knee as you lift helps you to achieve the right amount of speed in this move.

exercise 10 back extension, arms assist

• stability

a

b

This move should be performed very calmly. The amount of lift depends as much on the level of mobility in the spine as it does on your strength.

● Start with your feet shoulder width apart (or together if this is more comfortable). The ball should be on your abdominals rather than ribs. Rest your hands just in front of the top of the ball.
● Lift your chest off the ball by using a combination of lower back strength and some gentle assistance from the arms.
● Try to keep the legs in one set position, otherwise bending the knees will cancel out the extension you need the spine to move through.

!

tricks of the trade

I find that I need to give my clients the freedom to have their feet together or apart – it seems to be a comfort, rather than a functional, issue.

exercise 11 back extension, hands at head

● **stability** ● **strength**

a   b

Placing your hands at the side of your head means that you are now lifting them up, which makes the upper body feel heavier.

- The correct start position is achieved by having your legs straight and the toes firmly planted into the floor. The ball should be on your abdominals rather than ribs.
- Begin the move from a relaxed position lying over the ball to ensure that the fullest range of movement is achieved.
- This move is as much about the glute muscles as it is about the low back extensors, so as you reach the top of the movement ensure the buttocks are squeezed together firmly.

> ## tricks of the trade
> Note: Bending the knees might let you get a little bit higher, but it is cheating because the glutes and hip flexors are no longer fixing the pelvis. With the knees dropped down your start position is forward flexion meaning that the extra height is really coming from the hips rather than the spine.

exercise 12 back extension, arms extended

● stability ● strength ● power

a   b

- The correct start position is achieved by having your legs straight and the toes firmly planted into the floor. Your ball should be touching your abdominals rather than ribs.
- To achieve the correct arm position I find it better to have the two hands touching together as this tends to stop the arms 'waving' around.
- Extend your arms then lock them in position and lift the upper body off the ball.
- Avoid the temptation to gain extra height by bending the legs.

> **!**
>
> ### tricks of the trade
>
> I find a surprising number of clients hold their breath while performing this move, so I either ask them to stop doing this or keep them talking throughout the exercise – you simply can't hold your breath and talk at the same time.

exercise 13 quadruped hand raise

● **stability**

a   b

This move can really enhance mobility and stability in the shoulder girdle.

- The start position is very relaxed – most of your body weight is on the ball and your fingers and toes are providing some balance.
- Lift alternate arms up in a sweeping movement so that when you reach the top of the movement in your shoulder you then lift the chest off the ball.

> **! tricks of the trade**
> Keep your arms relaxed so that it looks like you are waving rather than punching.

exercise 14 quadruped leg raise

• stability • strength

a   b

Lifting your toes from the floor requires balance so practise this move through a small range of motion, then progress as your balance improves.

- The majority of your body weight is on the ball with your fingers and toes providing some balance points.
- Lift one foot, keeping the leg straight. Lift your foot as high as possible while maintaining control.
- Make sure you place your foot back onto the floor before lifting the opposite leg.

> **!**
>
> ### tricks of the trade
> When learning this move I find that letting my clients have their feet either together or apart helps to speed up the learning process – I don't want them to give up, so cutting them some slack makes sense.

exercise 15 quadruped hand and leg raise

• stability • strength • power

a   b

- The majority of your body weight should be on the ball, rather than your hands and feet.
- The aim is to lift the opposite hand and foot from the floor at the same time. To achieve this, think about pushing against the hand and the foot that remain on the ground rather than focusing on the limbs that are lifting, as this enhances balance and will also help you achieve more lift.

> **tricks of the trade**
>
> For some clients I find the biggest challenge of this move is the coordination. Practise the rhythm while standing up so when you get on the ball it is one less thing to think about.

exercise 16 standing Russian twist, ball against wall, feet apart

• stability

- Stand up against a wall, with the ball placed between your shoulders.
- Walk your feet a little further away from the wall, so that you are leaning back slightly, rather than standing upright. Your feet should be slightly apart for balance.
- Raise your arms to chest height, keeping the feet firmly planted, and rotate the upper body one way and then the other.
- Do this move slowly to begin with as you need to get used to the ball moving across the back of the shoulders.

tricks of the trade

Let the feet move – there is no need to keep them stuck solid to the floor. I always say the move should feel 'fluid', not 'frozen'.

exercise 17 standing Russian twist, ball against wall, feet together

• **stability**

With your feet together you will find that the range of movement is slightly less than when the feet are apart (in exercise 16).

- Stand up against a wall, with the ball placed between your shoulders.
- Walk your feet a little further away from the wall, so that you are leaning back slightly, rather than standing upright. Your feet should be together.
- Raise your arms to chest height, keeping the feet firmly planted, and rotate the upper body one way and then the other.
- Do this move slowly to begin with as you need to get used to the ball moving across the back of the shoulders.

tricks of the trade
Squeeze a rolled up towel between your knees if you have trouble keeping the lower body under control during this move.

exercise 18 Russian twist, arms across chest

● stability

a   b

- Start in a strong bridge position, with the knees, hips and shoulders horizontal to each other. The upper back should be the contact point with the ball.
- With your arms across your chest, the object of this move is not to create a huge amount of rotation, but rather to twist your body using pure strength rather than momentum.
- As you rotate, the ball will naturally roll away from the centre of your shoulders and towards your arms.
- Move slowly so that the effort is sustained rather than punchy.

! tricks of the trade

When I demonstrate this move to clients I often slip in a fake stumble just so that they can see that I don't expect them to be able to do this move perfectly first time – it also lets them see that personal trainers are only human.

exercise 19 Russian twist, arms raised, feet together

• stability • strength

a   b

- Start in a strong bridge position, with the knees, hips and shoulders horizontal to each other. The upper back should be the contact point with the ball.
- With your arms across your chest, the object of this move is not to create a huge amount of rotation, but rather to twist your body using pure strength rather than momentum.
- As you rotate, the ball will naturally move across your shoulders so it is important to balance speed with ability.
- Start with your arms in the highest position with the aim to move them through a 90-degree arch one way and then the other. The movement should be a smooth single action rather than 'punctuated'.

> ### tricks of the trade
> Don't let your eyes wander – keep your eye line at your hands rather than anything further away.

exercise 20 Russian twist, arms raised, feet apart

• **stability** • **strength** • **power**

This move is performed fast and therefore doesn't always look very neat.

- Start in a strong bridge position, with the knees, hips and shoulders horizontal to each other.
- The objective is to make the ball work really hard beneath you and this means the contact points with the ball will shift between your upper back, shoulders and, if you really attack it, the outside of the arms.
- Keep your feet at least shoulder width apart and bear in mind that the weight will be shifting between both feet rather than being evenly balanced.
- Unlike the slower versions of Russian twist the feet, knees and hips will be moving to generate the speed. Start with your arms in the highest position with the aim to move them through a 90-degree arch one way and then the other.

> **!** **tricks of the trade**
> This move is supposed to be fast and challenging and everybody rolls off the ball at some point. If you do, just sit down on the floor, reconnect with the ball and get straight back on.

exercise 21 lateral roll, ball behind shoulders

• **stability** • **strength**

a   b

This move evolved from the power version of the Russian twist (exercise 20), but the force comes from the legs rather than the torso, so the technique looks similar, but loses the rotation.

- Start in the bridge position (exercise 20) and put the arms out into a crucifix position.
- Move the ball beneath your shoulders by shifting your body (the force to get you moving is coming from your legs).
- When you shift your body from side to side your arms will become the contact point with the ball and therefore are load bearing.
- Start with small movements until you have mastered holding your weight in this way.

> ## tricks of the trade
> This is a difficult move so I only give it to clients that are ready. To help them through the first few repetitions I kneel behind the ball to make sure that it doesn't roll away. If you are training alone, simply put the ball near a wall.

exercise 22 plank, arms on ball, knees on floor

• **stability** • **strength**

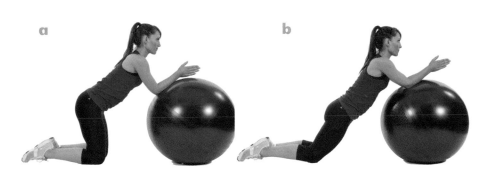

This position is very subtle and the intensity can change by slightly shifting the body position.

- Start with your body at an angle of 45 degrees to the floor, i.e. a straight line from the shoulder to hips and knees (remember, you should be kneeling on your knees). Your forearms provide the contact point with the ball.
- Hold this position.
- To change the intensity, change the distance between the knees and the ball – knees closer to the ball will make this move easier, while moving your knees further away will make it harder.

> **!**
>
> ### tricks of the trade
> This exercise is often just held in a static position for counts of 30 seconds plus. I, however, prefer to move in and out of the position and use deep breathing to multiply the benefits, so shift your weight forward and back so that you feel a distinct difference between loaded and unloaded.

exercise 23 plank, arms on ball, full body

• **stability** • **strength**

a   b

This move is often performed as a static exercise, however, I prefer to move in and out of the position and count the repetitions rather than just being still.

- Place your elbows on the ball then lift the knees off the ground, visualise a straight line from the shoulder to hips, knees and ankles.
- Hold the position for a single large breath in and out, then bend the knees to release the effort for a moment, then repeat.

> ! **tricks of the trade**
>
> When my clients go from the kneeling version of this to the harder straight leg version I make them start with their feet very wide apart, which helps with balance.

exercise 24 plank, arms on ball, alternate leg raise

• stability • strength • power

a   b

This move is often performed as a static exercise, however, I prefer to move in and out of the position and count the repetitions rather than just being still.

- The start position is a static plank, with your neck is in a neutral position. Visualise a straight line running through the shoulder, hips, knees and ankles.
- Breathe and lift one foot and hold.
- Lifting one foot increases the balance and strength demands, so practise maintaining good body alignment with a small leg raise, then introduce a higher leg raise.

tricks of the trade

Tall people can find this move hard. If it isn't working for you, rest your chest on the ball and perfect the leg lift, then when that feels natural pick up your body weight again.

exercise 25 plank, arms on ball, knee to ball

• **stability** • **strength** • **power**

a

b

To make this exercise achievable the arm position differs from the previous plank moves – your arms are wider and you'll need to grip the ball with them, rather than just resting them on top.

- The start position is a static plank, with your neck in a neutral position. Visualise a straight line running through the shoulder, hips, knees and ankles.
- Bring one knee at a time towards the ball, then lower back to the start position.
- Repeat with the other leg.

> **!**
>
> ## tricks of the trade
>
> The slower you go, the harder this is. When I demo this exercise I make sure that it doesn't look too neat so that my clients realise they have to go 'bang, bang' and get it over with.

exercise 26 plank, arms on ball, single side step

• **stability** • **strength** • **power**

- Start with your arms at shoulder width and grip the ball with them, rather than just resting them on top.
- The start position is a static plank, with your neck in a neutral position. Visualise a straight line running through the shoulder, hips, knees and ankles.
- Take a large step to one side, moving one foot at a time then, rather than returning to the centre position, take a large step to the other side.

! tricks of the trade

I would hate for you to waste your time so make sure that you set a target distance to which your feet must travel in every repetition, i.e. 50cm minimum.

exercise 27 plank, arms on ball, two foot split jump

• stability • strength • power

a   b

- Lie on the ball. Start with your arms at shoulder width and grip the ball with them, rather than just resting them on top.
- Bend your knees in what I describe as a 'ready' position.
- Jump the feet out and in.
- Extending the legs to straighten them would put unnecessary stress on the back, so keep the knees bent throughout.

> **!**
> ## tricks of the trade
> As this move is very assertive, to stop the ball getting away from you here's a trick that really works well: hold a small towel with both hands and it will help give you a better grip off the ball.

exercise 28 squat against wall

• stability

Only use a smooth wall and never do this against a door.

- Position the ball at the base of the spine and lean into the ball, knees bent. This not only secures the ball, but also gets you into an excellent position to work the glutes and hamstrings more than in a regular squat.
- Squat down until the ball rolls up to shoulder height, then stand up.

! **tricks of the trade**

In each of the squat moves squeezing a rolled up towel between the knees is great for making the hamstrings and glutes work harder.

---

exercise 29 squat against wall, arms raised

● **stability**

Only use a smooth wall and never do this against a door.

● Position the ball at the base of the spine and lean into the ball, knees bent. This not only secures the ball, but also gets you into an excellent position to work the glutes and hamstrings more than in a regular squat.
● Raise your arms above you so that they are in line with your ears.
● Squat down until the ball rolls up between your shoulders, then stand up.

> ## tricks of the trade
> As you really can't see how you are moving, I tell clients to keep the arms lifted so that they never come into your peripheral vision – if you see them, they are too low.

exercise 30 squat against wall, single leg

• stability • strength

Only use a smooth wall and never do this against a door. The reality of this move is that most of us cannot get as low in a single leg squat as we can when using both legs, so just accept that you won't be going down as low.

- Position the ball at the base of the spine and lean into the ball, knees bent. This not only secures the ball, but also gets you into an excellent position to work the glutes and hamstrings more than in a regular squat.
- Lift one foot from the floor and hold it out in front.
- Bend the supporting leg slowly and be ready for the fact that you will naturally lean to one side – try to resist this and keep the move straight up and down, rather than shifting to the side.
- Do all the repetitions on one side then change leg.

> **!**
>
> ## tricks of the trade
> Everybody seems to look at the leg that they are holding out in front when they perform single leg squats, which means they end up rounding the shoulders. Maybe it is because their personal trainer is also looking at their knee – I always say to let me look at the leg, while they should look straight ahead.

exercise 31 squat against wall, jump

• stability • strength • power

This move is all about the depth you can achieve by having the ball behind you, rather than the height that you will get from the jump section. Saying that, you will be surprised at how high you can get with that extra bit of contact the ball gives you.

- Position the ball at the base of the spine and lean into the ball, knees bent. This not only secures the ball, but also gets you into an excellent position to work the glutes and hamstrings more than in a regular squat.
- Squat down, pause for a moment then, while maintaining some pressure on the ball, jump up.
- Focus on the landing, as the moment you make contact with the ground your muscles are working to decelerate you and stop you ending up on the floor.

! tricks of the trade

I like to keep the reps very close together, so think of the landing as being a rebound rather than stopping between each repetition. Think to yourself: 'I want to get this over with quickly'.

exercise 32 ball against wall plank, knee raise, kick back

● stability ● strength

- Hold the ball against the wall at chest height with your forearms pushing against it.
- Your feet should be far enough from the wall to ensure that you have a sufficient pressure on the ball. You can tell if the feet are in the correct position because you will feel the abdominal muscles engage as you lean in.
- Raise one knee towards the ball, then swing the leg back. This dynamic movement will encourage the body to react and stabilise while the single leg stance will encourage strength.
- Do all the repetitions on one side then change to the other leg.

> **tricks of the trade**
> If there is any move that will highlight a lack of coordination, this is it. The ball adds to the challenge, so if my clients can't get the rhythm I start them off with their hands against the wall and introduce the ball when they are ready.

exercise 33 ball against wall, plank, leg swing

• **stability** • **strength**

- Hold the ball against the wall at chest height with your forearms pushing against it.
- Your feet should be far enough from the wall to ensure that you have a sufficient pressure on the ball. You can tell if the feet are in the correct position because you will feel the abdominal muscles engage as you lean in.
- Lift one leg up to the side (abduction) then swing it in front of the other leg (adduction).
- You will find that the better you get at this the more movement you will get through the spine and pelvis.

> ### tricks of the trade
> You will do better at this move if you don't lose focus on the ball – keep it squashed against the wall throughout the move.

exercise 34 ball against wall, press-up position, knee raise, kick back

• stability • strength

- Hold the ball against the wall at chest height with your arms almost straight pushing against it, rather than simply holding it.
- Your feet should be far enough from the wall to ensure that you have a sufficient pressure on the ball. You can tell if the feet are in the correct position because you will feel the abdominal muscles engage as you lean in.
- Also place your feet at shoulder width to prepare for when you lift one foot.
- Bring one knee up in front and aim to make contact with the ball, then swing the leg back, extending the hip.
- Do all the repetitions on one side then change legs.

tricks of the trade

If you are training on your own I bet after a few repetitions you are standing up straight with hardly any weight on the ball. I always use my foot or a line on the floor to keep the client's feet in the right place.

exercise 35 ball against wall, press-up position, leg swing

• stability • strength

- Hold the ball against the wall at chest height with your arms almost straight pushing against it, rather than simply holding it.
- Your feet should be far enough from the wall to ensure that you have a sufficient pressure on the ball. You can tell if the feet are in the correct position because you will feel the abdominal muscles engage as you lean in.
- Also place your feet at shoulder width to prepare for when you lift one foot.
- One leg swings out to the side (abduction) and then swings across in front of the other leg.
- It is too easy to just let the leg swing, so ensure that you are going through a full range of motion.
- Do all the repetitions on one side then change legs.

!

tricks of the trade

If you show me 50 people doing this exercise they will all look slightly different, so enjoy it and aim at least to have the same amount of swing from both legs.

exercise 36 ball against wall, press-up position, side step

• stability • strength • power

This move is deceptively hard, so increase the depth progressively.

- Push the ball against the wall at waist height, so that you feel that you are really pushing the ball into the wall rather than simply holding it up.
- Place your feet at shoulder width to prepare for when you lift one foot.
- Step out and load the leg, then step across the centre line of the body – it is perfectly fine to pivot the supporting foot rather than keeping it fixed on the floor.
- Do all the repetitions on one side then change legs.

tricks of the trade

If you don't set a target by the fourth or fifth rep your steps will be tiny. I always set the stride width target to at least 50cm – if my client is tall, it will be as much as 100cm.

exercise 37 ball against wall, press-up position, two foot jump

● **stability** ● **strength** ● **power**

This move is deceptively hard, so increase the depth progressively.

● Push the ball against the wall at waist height, so that you feel that you are really pushing the ball into the wall rather than simply holding it up.
● Place your feet at shoulder width to prepare.
● While pressing the ball hard against the wall jump your feet out and in.
● Don't feel you need to push your heels into the floor – being on the balls of the feet will give the move a much more aggressive dynamic feel.

tricks of the trade

Some moves have the potential to become very random – with this one if I think a client is just all over the place, I put a rolled up towel between their knees and make them jump without dropping it, which always calms things down (and takes the smile off their face).

exercise 38 ball against wall, press-up position, high impact run-push

● **stability** ● **strength** ● **power**

You can create a number of different 'feels' to this move by changing the height that you hold the ball at – hold it low and you will feel it in the abdominals, hold it higher to feel more muscle activity in the chest and shoulders.

● Push the ball against the wall, so that you feel that you are really pushing the ball into the wall rather than simply holding it up.
● Place your feet at shoulder width to prepare.
● Standing on the balls of the feet press the ball hard into the wall then run.

> **! tricks of the trade**
>
> Honestly, if you can do this for more than 1 minute, you are a superhero! I like to tell my clients that when they do this move flat out they are going faster than any treadmill, so be happy if you last 45 seconds.

exercise 39 press-up, hands on floor, ball at knees

● **stability** ● **strength**

a b

You will often find in this position that you cannot get the same amount of depth in the press-up that can be achieved when the ball is further away from the hands. Just accept this, as this is the way the shoulders move.

● Lie prone (face down) on the ball, starting from behind the ball and rolling over the top until your knees are the main contact point.
● Place your hands at shoulder width and bend the arms to perform a press-up.
● Let the entire body pivot on the ball rather than simply hinging from the waist.

> ## tricks of the trade
> This move is hard at both ends of the body. To make it more achievable for new clients I will put their hands on a step so that their upper body is higher at the start of the move – this really helps with building confidence to bend the elbows.

exercise 40 press-up, hands on floor, ball at shins

• stability • strength

a   b

For this press up lowering the body so that you have an approximately 90-degree bend at the elbows is the target for a good range of motion. If you exceed this, you will find that the challenge comes more from lack of mobility in the shoulders rather than strength.

- Lie prone (face down) on the ball, starting from behind the ball and rolling over the top until your shins are the main contact point.
- Place your hands at shoulder width and bend the arms to perform a press-up.
- Let the entire body pivot on the ball rather than simply hinging from the waist.

> **tricks of the trade**
> This move falls apart if you lift your head up. I get my clients to visualise a line drawn between their two thumbs and to keep looking at that throughout this exercise.

exercise 41 press-up, hands on floor, ball at feet

● **stability** ● **strength**

a  b

- Lie prone (face down) on the ball, starting from behind the ball and rolling over the top until your feet are the main contact point. Keep your legs straight. Because the hands and feet are such a distance from each other, stabilising the ball becomes the first challenge.
- Place your hands at shoulder width and, once you have gained composure, bend the arms to perform a press-up.
- Let the entire body pivot on the ball rather than simply hinging from the waist.
- As soon as your upper body drops below the feet this move becomes a challenge, so build up your range of motion as you increase your confidence.

tricks of the trade

Let the ball move and, unless you are superhuman, the best part of the foot to have in contact with the ball is the top of your foot rather than your toes.

exercise 42 press-up, hands on ball, knees on floor

• stability

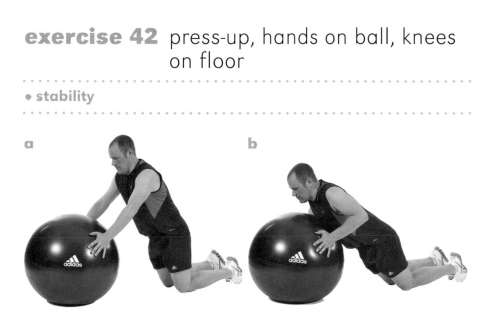

a   b

- Kneeling and facing the ball grip the section of the ball in front of you, rather than on top of the ball.
- Set the body position so that there is a straight line from the shoulder to hips and knees, then bend the elbows to perform the press-up, maintaining the straight body position throughout the movement.

! tricks of the trade

New clients always think they have to touch the ball with their head on this one. Just bend the arms to 90 degrees, thank you, and leave the heading to footballers!

exercise 43 press-up, hands on ball, full body, feet apart

• stability • strength

a   b

- Grip the ball with your hands at shoulder width and step your feet apart. The wider your foot position, the easier the press will be, as you are effectively shortening the distance between the two contact points of the ball and floor.
- Set your body position so there is a straight line from your shoulders to knees, and bend your elbows with the aim of touching your chest to the ball – don't, however, 'bounce' your chest on the ball; use your strength, not recoil.

> **!**
>
> ### tricks of the trade
> The goal is to eventually be able to do great press-ups, and if that means you need to bend your knees a little to start with, just do it. The art of keeping people motivated is knowing when to compromise and when it is right to push them hard.

exercise 44 press-up, hands on ball, feet together

• stability • strength

a   b

- Grip the ball with your hands at shoulder width apart.
- Set your body position so that there is a line from your shoulders through your hips and down to your knees. Maintain this position as you bend your arms until your chest touches the ball.
- Press back up using strength rather than building up momentum and bouncing off the ball.

tricks of the trade

This really works – rather than pushing into the ball as you go up and down, try to squeeze the hands together. If you get it right it will feel like you are hugging an invisible person.

exercise 45 pike, feet on ball, hands on floor

• **stability** • **strength**

a   b

- Lie prone (face down) on the ball with your hands out in front.
- Walk your hands forward until the contact point with the ball is the top of your thighs. Place your hands on the floor.
- While keeping your arms straight, lift your hips up so that your body forms a triangle with the floor (the ball will have rolled from the thighs to the shins).
- Slowly reverse the action and repeat.

> ## tricks of the trade
>
> Everybody tries to do this using just their leg strength – the eureka moment for my clients is when they work from the shoulders and chest as well as the legs.

exercise 46 bridge, ball touching upper back, knees very bent

• stability

a   b

- Start by leaning against the ball with it between your shoulder blades – this contact point stays the same throughout the move.
- Keeping your knees bent lift the hips up so that at the top of the movement the knees are at 90 degrees.
- Try to make it so that the ball stays still and the body is moving, rather than letting the ball roll away from its start position.

> ## tricks of the trade
>
> People think they need to look neat when they do this move so they tuck their hands in to their sides. It is much better to let the hands hang down to the floor, as if you are struggling with balance, this will help.

exercise 47 bridge, ball touching upper back, legs extended

• stability • strength

a   b

- Start with the ball between your shoulders then step your feet away from the ball – don't just straighten the legs completely because you will just be fighting to stay on the ball.
- Keep your knees slightly bent and use both heels as the contact point.
- Your arms make a big difference to balance on this move, so while you are learning hold your arms out to assist balance. Ultimately, though, you should aim to have them closer to the body.

> ## tricks of the trade
>
> No matter how well I teach it, this move confuses some clients because they can't work out which muscles are making things happen. The best way to overcome this is to focus on everything that is 'behind you', so your hamstrings and glutes are the prime movers and everything else is the support act.

exercise 48 bridge, lying on floor, knees very bent, arms wide

• stability • strength

a   b

For many people this move produces a lot of movement from the ball, which is a good thing because movement of the ball is highly productive and should be encouraged.

- Place your heels on the ball, not right on top, but close.
- With your palms down press your hands against the floor.
- Then, using your legs and glutes, lift your hips from the ground.

tricks of the trade

I find this exercise can look untidy because at the top of the move you are only making contact with the heels and back of the shoulders and the chances are the ball will be wobbling. To overcome this don't think about the ball – just focus on keeping a straight line from the chin down through the ribs to the pelvis.

exercise 49 bridge, lying on floor, legs near straight, arms wide

• stability • strength

a   b

There is always the temptation with this move to get to the top then just give up – don't: lower the body back down to the ground with control. A positive by-product of this move is that you get a lot of muscle activity in the upper body, as it struggles to combat the ball's desire to roll away when you lift the hips.

- Place your heels nearly on the top of the ball, then lift your hips from the floor.
- The arms remain stretched out wide throughout the exercise so the body forms the shape of a cross
- The ultimate position is to maintain a straight line from your ankles to your lower ribs.

tricks of the trade

The reason the arms are wide is to help with balance, but you can add to muscle activity by placing your palms flat and pressing really hard against the floor.

exercise 50 bridge, lying on floor, knees very bent, arms by side

• stability • strength

a   b

Not having the arms wide seems like a subtle change to this movement, but it significantly increases the need for balance.

- Place your heels nearly on the top of the ball, keeping your knees bent.
- With your palms down press the hands against the floor, the hands stay on the floor throughout but avoid using them to push up, they are simply there to assist balance, or for an added challenge lift the hands off the floor as shown above.
- Press your feet against the ball and lift your hips off the ground, lift as high as you can then, lower back down to the floor

> ## tricks of the trade
> I find that this exercise can look untidy because at the top of the move you are only making contact with the heels on the ball and back of the shoulders on the floor and the chances are the ball will be wobbling. But persevere with it – the trick is to try and push the ball away from you slightly as well as lifting the hips straight up. Build up the range of motion gradually – it's all about quality.

exercise 51 bridge, lying on floor, legs near straight, no hands

● **stability** ● **strength**

When you do this move for the first time you will find that you want to use your hands, but avoid using them by keeping the range of movement small until you have built up your balance and muscle control.

- Place your heels near the top of the ball (your head, shoulders and heels will be the only contact points when you have lifted). Your arms and hands are lifted off the floor and remain close to your sides.
- Lift up your hips until you ultimately have a straight line from the ankles to the base of the ribs.
- Lower down under control – it is tempting to just let go, but this move is all about quality, not drama.

!

tricks of the trade

I find that clients who lift up slowly don't really feel much happening, so there is only one thing for it: don't just lift, but thrust.

gym ball stretches

I have two different modes when I stretch:

1 If I am actively trying to increase my flexibility (stretch mode), I am going to take the position to the point of discomfort, hold it then keep going a little further.
2 When I am chilled out (relax mode), I just get into positions that are comfortable and enjoy the moment.

The following stretches are a combination of both. There are many other stretches that you can use with the ball, but I find that many of them incorporate the ball for the sake of it, and that you are often better off doing a similar stretch on the floor. This selection uses the ball to enhance the stretch, rather than just using it as an accessory.

When doing any of the workouts I suggest using all of these stretches at the end of the session. There are two versions of the chest stretch and two versions of the down dog – choose just one of each.

exercise 52 chest stretch, lying on back

- Perform this stretch in relax mode (see page 99).
- Rest your shoulders and head on the ball, reach your arms out to the side and let the weight instigate a stretch through your chest, deltoids and deep into the ribs.
- To make this stretch effective it is important to position yourself on the ball so that you have lots of control. This way you will be able to relax into the stretch rather than fighting against balance issues.
- For added effect try taking some deep breaths.
- Hold this position for at least 20 seconds or preferably longer.

> **! tricks of the trade**
>
> We personal trainers always like to look busy, but I avoid trying to help clients on this move by stretching their arms back. The range of movement is limited by the joints, not by tight muscles.

exercise 53 chest stretch, one hand on ball

- Perform this stretch in stretch mode (see page 99).
- Position the ball to one side and place the arm you wish to stretch on top of it.
- Gently lean towards the ball. In doing so you will feel a stretch through your chest and shoulders.
- Either roll in and out of the stretch for a gentle dynamic stretch or simply hold the position for 20 seconds for a static stretch.

tricks of the trade

Shoulder joints and muscles are not like hinges on a door, rather they move in multiple directions, so push the ball around in small circles, which helps to really loosen up through the shoulder and chest.

exercise 54 down dog, knees on floor

- Perform this stretch in relax mode (see page 99).
- Kneel behind the ball and place your hands firmly in front of you, rather than on top of the ball.
- Push your hips backward and let your head fall through your arms and towards the floor.
- When you reach the point that you feel the stretch working hold the position and take some deep breaths, which will intensify the stretch.

> **!**
>
> ### tricks of the trade
> A stretch is supposed to be a time of relaxation as well as action so if you struggle to keep the ball still simply stop it moving by putting it against a wall so that you can concentrate on your muscles rather than the ball.

exercise 55 down dog, standing, hands on ball

- Perform this stretch in stretch mode (see page 99).
- Kneel behind the ball and place your hands on the ball, slightly towards you rather than on top.
- Apply pressure to the ball and straighten your legs until your heels touch the ground (while this is a normal range of motion for many people, tight calf muscles make this a challenge so accept that you may need to build up to the full range).
- With your arms and legs straight, let your head hang between your arms. A good visualisation is that you are forming an inverted 'V' shape with your body.
- Breathe deep and either hold the position or move in and out of the posture.

tricks of the trade

Patience, patience, patience. This is a fabulous stretch but some of you will find it a challenge to keep the arms and legs straight - persevere, it really is worth it.

exercise 56 hip flexor

This movement is great because the hip flexors are made up of multiple muscles and therefore respond better to the various positions.

- Perform this stretch in stretch mode (see page 99).
- Place the ball next to you so that you can lean into it and move in and out of the stretch.
- If the ball is on your left then take the left leg back. Ensure the knee of your front leg stays behind the ankle. This will encourage a deeper more satisfying stretch in the hamstring on the front leg and a very targeted stretch in the hip flexors of your rear leg.

> **!**
>
> ### tricks of the trade
> The ball really changes this stretch for many people from being something they struggle with into an enjoyable, productive stretch. Some clients even go as far as saying it feels nice. If they do, it is probably time to extend their back leg more.

exercise 57 full body supine

This stretch could be mistaken for merely 'lying' on the ball, however it does actually require a good level of balance and coordination, especially if you are very relaxed with your eyes closed.

- You can control what muscles are stretched specifically by applying subtle pressure through the feet.
- Support your head with the ball. The perfect scenario is that you need to feel your body weight being taken by the ball, rather than your feet. This takes time, but eventually you can reach the point that it feels like you are floating on the ball.

tricks of the trade

This feels so good that I want everybody to be able to enjoy it, so if your balance is poor, put your toes against a wall and you will feel as if you have suddenly switched it on.

gym ball moves with dumbbells

When using a gym ball and dumbbells together the reality is that you have to treat the effects of the weights differently than if you were doing the same moves on a solid bench. The rules that apply when mixing weights and a ball are simple:

- Check that your body weight and the dumbbells combined do not exceed the maximum capacity of the ball.
- Ensure that with the selected weight you can get on and off the ball safely, even when you are tired.
- Finally, consider using less weight on the ball than you would on a bench (approximately 10–20 per cent less then you would use on a solid surface). The aim when using the ball is for more subtle effects than we get using a bench. A ball is not the place to think about lifting your maximum weights.

getting on and off the ball with weights

Having coached and observed many thousands of people using a ball and weights together I have developed a standard approach to getting on and off the ball that involves the minimum of fuss.

- If the exercise is to be performed in the supine position (face-up), I sit on the ball and pick up the weights before getting into the start position of the exercise.
- If the exercise is to be performed in the prone position (face down), I will place the weights within easy reach, lie on the ball in the start position and then pick up the dumbbells.

exercise 58 chest press, feet apart

● stability ● strength

- Start with the ball between your shoulders and your legs and torso in a bridge position.
- Begin with the weights in the up position so that your arms are straight, the weights are above your chest rather than head.
- The wide foot position will not only assist you slightly with the balance challenge, but it also encourages the muscles in the pelvic floor to work.
- Lower the weights until they reach chest height then press them back up to the start position.

> **tricks of the trade**
> As soon as you start moving your arms you will forget about your legs. Imagine you have a glass of water resting on your tummy – if you drop your hips, the water will spill.

exercise 59 chest press, feet together

• stability • strength

a   b

- Begin with the ball between your shoulders and your legs and torso in a bridge position (aim for a straight line from shoulders through to ankles).
- Having the feet together makes the bridge position more challenging from the start, so if you do feel like you are losing control, simply drop the hips to the floor, regain control and start again.
- Start with the weights in the up position so that your arms are straight, lower them until they reach chest height, then push them up again ready for the next repetition.

> **!**
>
> ### tricks of the trade
> You should be squeezing your glute muscles tightly during this exercise.

exercise 60 chest press, alternate arms, feet apart

• stability • strength

a
b

With all alternating arm moves there is a natural progression from moving one arm at a time (a punching action) to having both arms moving at the same time (a sawing action). The rest of the technique should stay the same with the addition of the sawing movement causing more activity within the core.

- Begin with the ball between your shoulders and your legs and torso in a bridge position (aim for a straight line from shoulders through to ankles).
- Having your feet apart will help you with the balance challenge, however, when you press with just one arm you will feel the muscles of the opposite inner thigh working hard – this is good.
- Starting with the weights in the up position so that your arms are straight, lower one weight. As you reach the maximum range of motion from the shoulder, roll your body weight on the ball towards the same side.
- Press the weight back up at the same time as rolling your body back into the start position and repeat with the other side.

> **!**
> ### tricks of the trade
> I always like to progress my clients in stages, so make sure you have perfected the single arm action before progressing to the double arm move.

exercise 61 chest press, alternate arms, feet together

• stability • strength

a   b

- Begin with the ball between your shoulders and your legs and torso in a bridge position (aim for a straight line from shoulders through to ankles).
- Having your feet together means as soon as you move the weight your body will want to move away from the 'centre line'. This is fine, however, you need to take control of the movement rather than letting the ball take you where it wants.
- Start with the dumbbells in the up position so that your arms are straight then lower one down and press it up again before moving the other.

> **tricks of the trade**
>
> If you only have a limited range of weights available to use but want to enhance the challenge, try this move with you eyes closed – it makes you feel as if somebody switched off your coordination.

exercise 62 dumbbell fly

● stability ● strength

There are lots of variables that can be applied to the dumbbell fly move, most very subtle. You can shift the contact points slightly and move the weights through a slightly different plane of motion, however, the principles of the movement stay the same.

● The contact point with the ball is just below your scapular (shoulder blades) – this ensures that your body weight is not restricting the free movement of these joints. Make sure your feet are flat on the floor and your knees are bent to a 90-degree angle.
● Start with the weights in the up position so that your arms are straight. Open the arms to perform the fly movement (i.e. arms straight out to the side at shoulder height).
● The critical point is at the bottom of the move – you need to smoothly transition from the down to up phase. There is a temptation to bounce your body weight against the ball at this point, but avoid this if you can.

> ## tricks of the trade
> As you may not be using the heaviest weight that you can cope with, slightly alter the line of each arm rep.

111

exercise 63 dumbbell fly, toes lifted

● **stability** ● **strength** ● **power**

The reason for lifting the toes is to create more muscle activation throughout the entire body, which occurs because you are working on the smallest possible contact point. When you first attempt this move you will be aware of a significant amount of muscle activity in the hamstrings, glutes and adductors, which is something you would never get when performing a fly on a bench.

- The contact point with the ball is just below your scapular (shoulder blades) – this ensures that your body weight is not restricting the free movement of the moving joints.
- In the start position, your feet begin flat on the floor and as you lift the weights above you lift your toes off the floor so that you are resting just on your heels (try to maintain this position until you have done the last repetition).
- Start with the weights in the up position so that your arms are straight, open the arms to perform the fly movement (i.e. arms straight out to the side at shoulder height).
- Lower the weights under control and then work against the resistance on the way back up.

> **tricks of the trade**
> This move looks so innocent until you try it. When the client's balance is all over the place, you can quickly fix this by asking them to squeeze a towel between their knees.

exercise 64 bent over fly, sitting on front of ball

• stability • strength

a

b

There are a number of variables that can be changed to create different versions of this move, however, they are subtle and therefore can be experimented with once you have have mastered this classic version.

- Sit on the front of the ball, knees bent comfortably. Bend over from the hips.
- Hold the dumbbells with arms straight. The weights will either be in line with your feet or just behind them (your flexibility governs this; if you are flexible you will normally be able to extend the feet further in front of you).
- Start by having your shoulders rounded to enable you to retract the scapular through its fullest range of motion against resistance. Raise the weights in a smooth arc, breathing out on the lift and then smoothly return them to the start position.

! tricks of the trade

When I work with clients I try to only change one variable at a time, which could be changing your position on the ball (top or front), changing the position of your feet (forward or back) and altering the plane of motion that the weights travel through (straight up or slightly forward and back).

113

exercise 65 fly with sit-up

• stability • strength • power

a   b

It is really important not to get carried away with this move and to keep contact with the ball at all times –if you lose contact, it may roll away from you when you sit back down.

- The contact point with the ball is just below your scapular (shoulder blades) – this ensures that your body weight is not restricting the free movement of these joints.
- Place your feet shoulder width apart, then for the first repetition lower the weight outwards in a fly motion.
- On the way back up swiftly bring the weights forwards and sit up at the same time, you will now be sat up with your arms in front of you (similar to as if you were about to dive into a swimming pool).
- Reverse the move by rolling back onto the ball.

> **tricks of the trade**
>
> I always get clients to practise this move without the weights before they try it with lumps of metal in their hands.

exercise 66 reverse fly, weights in front of ball

● stability ● strength

Practise this move without the weights first, so that you get a good feel for the range of movement that could be achieved when holding the weights. Learn it, then work it.

- The correct start position is important with this move: aim to have the contact point with the ball on your abdominals rather than on the ribs, as this will enable you to move freely during the exercise.
- Place the weight in front of the ball and get yourself into a comfortable start position.
- Your toes are the contact point with the floor and your feet should be hip width apart.
- Hold the weights and extend your back until your arms are straight and the weights are lifted from the floor.
- With a fly movement, lift the arms out and up and continue lifting until you have fully retracted the scapular.
- Lower the weights back down under control rather than just letting them go.

! tricks of the trade

Even relatively strong people can be weak through this plane of motion, so to avoid embarrassment I start clients with a lighter weight than usual – it's always better to be able say, 'Let's go heavier', rather than, 'Oh dear – that is too heavy'.

---

exercise 67 pull over, dumbbell full range

• stability • strength

a
b

Depending upon your height, the weight of your arms alone may challenge you while performing this move, so I always have people practise this move without weights before adding the extra challenge of resistance.

- The contact point with the ball is just below your scapular (shoulder blades) – this ensures that your body weight is not restricting the free movement of moving joints.
- Start with the weights in the up position so that your arms are straight and your feet are hip width apart.
- Keeping the weights close together, but not touching, lower them towards the floor behind your head through a smooth arc. When you reach the limitation of your range, your hips might lift slightly, which is fine.
- Using your chest, shoulders and abdominals lift the weights back up to the start position.

> **!** **tricks of the trade**
>
> An option with this move is to perform it with a single weight rather than a pair, however, I personally like the fact that with two weight the hands are not locked together and therefore more muscle activity has to occur.

exercise 68 pull over, dumbbell full range, sit-up

• stability • strength • power

a   b

Practise this move without the weights, and when you feel you have mastered the coordination, add the weights.

- Start with your body in a bridge position, with the contact point with the ball in the middle of your spine, rather than pressing on the shoulder blades.
- Hold the weights above you and for the first repetition lower the dumbbells behind you in a smooth arc.
- Then, when you reach the bottom of the movement, speed the action up and aim for the weight to go between the legs and towards the ball, but don't hit the ball!
- Make sure that you keep contact with the ball at all times in the middle of your spine.
- As you decelerate the weights reverse the movement and roll back down onto the ball, going through the same arc movement.

! tricks of the trade

Even a small weight can build up a lot of momentum during this exercise and smashing weights into the floor is not cool. Make sure your hands are dry before you start this exercise – dumbbells flying across a room is never funny.

3 training with a gym ball

how to use the gym ball training sessions

- -

As people become more experienced in training with a gym ball there is a temptation to forego a formal training plan and work through a session training body parts randomly. This can be effective, but human nature dictates that, given the opportunity, we often end up focusing on the parts we like to work rather than the parts we need to work.

The training sessions in this section follow the S.A.F.E. philosophy of progression and are divided into the three basic facets of this system: stability, strength and power. They are sequenced in such a way that if you were an absolute beginner when you started, you should have at least 18 months of progressive exercise experience before you perform the hardest session. So, a novice would first attempt the 15 minute stability session followed, when ready, by the 30 minute and then 45 minute sessions. This process could take three to six months. When the stability sessions have been mastered and no longer present a significant challenge, the 15 minute strength session can be attempted followed, when ready, by the 30 and 45 minute sessions; again, this process could take three to six months. Having developed stability and strength over this length of time the body will be well prepared to progress to the power sessions, which follow the same logical progressions. Note: The timings are approximate and include a short warm-up and stretching at the end of the session.

The reality is, of course, that many people are not complete beginners, so Table 2 gives you an idea of where to start depending upon your experience and physical ability.

Table 3 Assessing which training session to begin with	
Stage	**Where to start**
You have not used a gym ball on a regular basis	If so that makes you a novice – start with the stability sessions before progressing to strength then power
You have been using a gym ball for 6–18 months and can do a perfect overhead squat	If so that makes you experienced – you might benefit from doing the stability sessions, but you can start with the strength sessions before progressing to the power sessions
You have been using a gym ball for 18 months or more and can do a perfect overhead squat	If so, you might benefit from doing the stability and strength sessions, but you can start with the power sessions.

the warm-up

Before you start any of the workouts, you need to do a warm-up. This can vary depending upon where you are – in a gym you might choose to use the cardio equipment (treadmill, rower, cross trainer) to get ready. This is fine, however, I find the most effective warm-up is one that specifically mimics the work that is just about to be done, so I like to prepare by going through movements that feature in the actual workout, e.g. full range versions of light squats, rotation and shoulder movements, along with some temperature-raising activity such as jogging on the spot.

post-workout stretch

In the world of fitness we habitually stretch at the end of our workout sessions when the muscles are still warm. However, muscles will also be fatigued and therefore not particularly receptive to being stretched. The reality is that most people just want to get out of the door when they have finished the work section, and they view stretching as something that delays their shower, so I like to do the essential stretches just after the workout then make time when less fatigued to do some more quality, focused flexibility work.

The effects of stretching are cumulative so don't expect miracles the first time, or if you really struggle to make time for them, remember that the reason for warming up and stretching at the end of every session is to reduce the risk of injury. So, make a habit of incorporating stretching into your workout, or risk paying for the privilege of a physiotherapist telling you the same thing in the future.

You should complete the following essential stretches at the end of every gym ball session (see below). Hold each of the stretches for at least 20 seconds and try to relax and enjoy them.

Stretch 1 lower leg

Stretch 2 front and rear upper leg

Stretch 3 chest

Stretch 4 upper back

Stretch 5 shoulders

stability workout sessions

15 minute stability (15 reps per move ● 1 set ● 1 circuit)	
Order in which to do moves	**Technique**
exercise 1 sit-up arms at waist (page 48)	
exercise 10 back extension, arms assist (page 57)	
exercise 28 squat against wall (page 75)	
exercise 46 bridge, ball touching upper back, knees very bent (page 93)	
exercise 13 quadruped hand raise (page 60)	
exercise 34 ball against wall, press-up position, knee raise kick back (page 81)	

exercise 7 seated pelvic tilt (page 54)	
exercise 42 press-up, hands on ball, knees on floor (page 89)	
exercise 4 sit-up rotation, feet apart (page 51)	
exercise 18 Russian twist, arms across chest (page 65)	

30 minute stability (15 reps per move ● 1 set ● 1 circuit)	
Order in which to do moves	**Technique**
exercise 48 bridge, lying on floor, knees very bent, arms wide (page 95)	
exercise 16 standing Russian twist, ball against wall, feet apart (page 63)	
exercise 22 plank, arms on ball, knees on floor (page 69)	
exercise 28 squat against wall (page 75)	
exercise 2 sit-up hands at head (page 49)	
exercise 42 press-up, hands on ball, knees on floor (page 89)	

exercise 7 seated pelvic tilt (page 54)	
exercise 35 ball against wall, press-up position, leg swing (page 82)	
exercise 10 back extension, arms assist (page 57)	
exercise 4 sit-up rotation, feet apart (page 51)	
exercise 13 quadruped hand raise (page 60)	
exercise 46 bridge, ball touching upper back, knees very bent (page 93)	
exercise 33 ball against wall plank, leg swing (page 80)	

exercise 17 standing Russian twist, ball against wall, feet together (page 64)	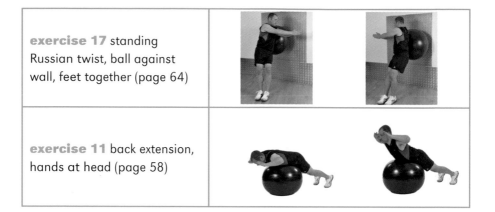
exercise 11 back extension, hands at head (page 58)	

45 minute stability (15 reps per move ● 1 set ● 2 circuits)	
Order in which to do moves	**Technique**
exercise 22 plank, arms on ball, knees on floor (page 69)	
exercise 42 press-up, hands on ball, knees on floor (page 89)	
exercise 28 squat against wall (page 75)	
exercise 35 ball against wall, press-up position, leg swing (page 82)	

exercise 4 sit-up rotation, feet apart (page 51)	
exercise 7 seated pelvic tilt (page 54)	
exercise 46 bridge, ball touching upper back, knees very bent (page 93)	
exercise 17 standing Russian twist, ball against wall, feet together (page 64)	
exercise 33 ball against wall plank, leg swing (page 80)	
exercise 11 back extension, hands at head (page 58)	
exercise 13 quadruped hand raise (page 60)	

exercise 10 back extension, arms assist (page 57)	

strength workout sessions

15 minute strength (10 reps per move ● 2 sets ● 1 circuit)	
Order in which to do moves	**Technique**
exercise 2 sit-up hands at head (page 49)	
exercise 29 squat against wall, arms raised (page 76)	
exercise 14 quadruped leg raise (page 61)	
exercise 19 Russian twist, arms raised, feet together (page 66)	

exercise 23 plank, arms on ball, full body (page 70)	
exercise 11 back extension, hands at head (page 58)	
exercise 32 ball against wall plank, knee raise, kick back (page 79)	
exercise 49 bridge, lying on floor, legs near straight, arms wide (page 96)	
exercise 8 sit-up knee raise, feet apart (page 55)	
exercise 30 squat against wall, single leg (page 77)	

30 minute strength (10 reps per move ● 2 sets ● 1 circuit)	
Order in which to do moves	**Technique**
exercise 39 press-up, hands on floor, ball at knees (page 86)	
exercise 47 bridge, ball touching upper back, legs extended (page 94)	
exercise 5 sit-up, rotation, feet together (page 52)	
exercise 21 lateral roll, ball behind shoulders (page 68)	
exercise 45 pike, feet on ball, hands on floor (page 92)	
exercise 50 bridge, lying on floor, knees very bent, arms by side (page 97)	

exercise 2 sit-up hands at head (page 49)	
exercise 19 Russian twist, arms raised, feet together (page 66)	
exercise 30 squat against wall, single leg (page 77)	
exercise 32 ball against wall plank, knee raise, kick back (page 79)	
exercise 35 ball against wall, press-up position, leg swing (page 82)	
exercise 7 seated pelvic tilt (page 54)	
exercise 28 squat against wall (page 75)	

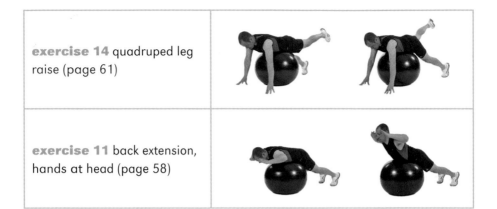

| exercise **14** quaduped leg raise (page 61) | |
| exercise **11** back extension, hands at head (page 58) | |

45 minute strength (10 reps per move ● 3 sets ● 1 circuit)	
Order in which to do moves	**Technique**
exercise **45** pike, feet on ball, hands on floor (page 92)	
exercise **5** sit-up, rotation, feet together (page 52)	
exercise **47** bridge, ball touching upper back, legs extended (page 94)	
exercise **19** Russian twist, arms raised, feet together (page 66)	

exercise 28 squat against wall (page 75)	
exercise 7 seated pelvic tilt (page 54)	
exercise 21 lateral roll, ball behind shoulders (page 68)	
exercise 39 press-up, hands on floor, ball at knees (page 86)	
exercise 2 sit-up hands at head (page 49)	
exercise 35 ball against wall, press-up position, leg swing (page 82)	
exercise 32 ball against wall plank, knee raise, kick back (page 79)	

exercise 50 bridge, lying on floor, knees very bent, arms by side (page 97)	
exercise 36 ball against wall, press-up position, side step (page 83)	
exercise 30 squat against wall, single leg (page 77)	
exercise 14 quadruped leg raise (page 61)	

power workout sessions

15 minute power (8 reps per move ● 2 sets ● 1 circuit min. 15 second recovery between moves)

Order in which to do moves	Technique
exercise 3 sit-up arms extended (page 50)	
exercise 12 back extension, arms extended (page 59)	
exercise 31 squat against wall, jump (page 78)	
exercise 20 Russian twist, arms raised, feet apart (page 67)	
exercise 24 plank, arms on ball, alternate leg raise (page 71)	
exercise 15 quadruped hand and leg raise (page 62)	

135

exercise 36 ball against wall, press-up position, side step (page 83)	
exercise 45 pike, feet on ball, hands on floor (page 92)	
exercise 51 bridge, lying on floor, legs near straight, no hands (page 98)	
exercise 25 plank, arms on ball, knee to ball (page 72)	

30 minutes power (8 reps per move ● 3 sets ● 1 circuit min. 15 second recovery between moves)

Order in which to do moves	Technique
exercise 27 plank, arms on ball, two foot split jump (page 74)	
exercise 38 ball against wall, press-up position, high impact run-push (page 85)	

exercise 31 squat against wall, jump (page 78)	
exercise 6 sit-up reach, toe touch (page 53)	
exercise 40 press-up, hands on floor, ball at shins (page 87)	
exercise 37 ball against wall, press-up position, two foot jump (page 84)	
exercise 24 plank, arms on ball, alternate leg raise (page 71)	
exercise 36 ball against wall, press-up position, side step (page 83)	
exercise 9 sit-up knee raise, feet together (page 56)	

exercise 26 plank, arms on ball, single side step (page 73)	
exercise 29 squat against wall, arms raised (page 76)	
exercise 3 sit-up arms extended (page 50)	
exercise 20 Russian twist, arms raised, feet apart (page 67)	
exercise 15 quadruped hand and leg raise (page 62)	

45 minutes power (12 reps per move ● 3 sets ● 1 circuit min. 15 second recovery between moves)

Order in which to do moves	Technique
exercise 36 ball against wall, press-up position, side step (page 83)	

exercise 38 ball against wall, press-up position, high impact run-push (page 85)	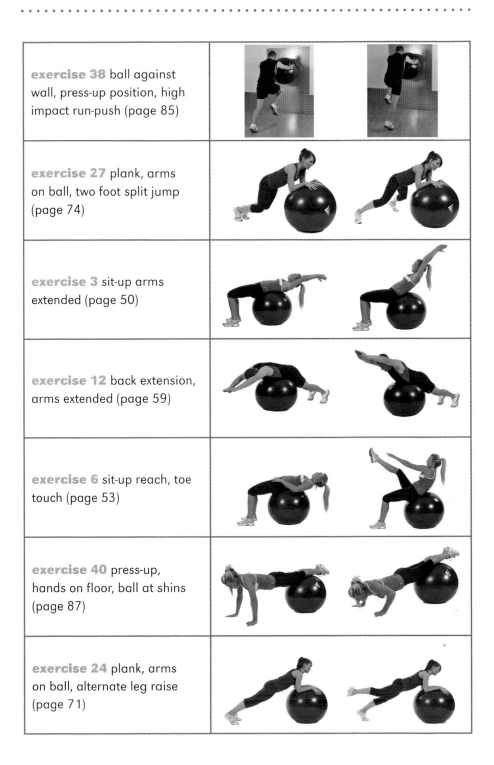
exercise 27 plank, arms on ball, two foot split jump (page 74)	
exercise 3 sit-up arms extended (page 50)	
exercise 12 back extension, arms extended (page 59)	
exercise 6 sit-up reach, toe touch (page 53)	
exercise 40 press-up, hands on floor, ball at shins (page 87)	
exercise 24 plank, arms on ball, alternate leg raise (page 71)	

exercise 15 quadruped hand and leg raise (page 62)	
exercise 31 squat against wall, jump (page 78)	
exercise 26 plank, arms on ball, single side step (page 73)	
exercise 44 press-up, hands on ball, feet together (page 91)	
exercise 51 bridge, lying on floor, legs near straight, no hands (page 98)	
exercise 20 Russian twist, arms raised, feet apart (page 67)	

and finally...

The gym ball has in a very short time, gone from being something that few people had ever used to being one of the most popular items of fitness equipment for home and gymnasiums. The possibilities are endless, and no matter what your goals, a gym ball can play a significant part in helping you to achieve them.

Whether you are a personal trainer, sportsperson or fitness enthusiast, I hope you are now fully equipped to get the most out of the valuable time you spend doing exercise with your gym ball, a most versatile and dynamic piece of equipment. All I ask is that you use all the information I have given in this book and make it part of an integrated health and fitness-driven lifestyle. My many thousands of hours spent in gymnasiums, health clubs, sport fields and with personal training clients has taught me that, given the chance, people like to do the things they are already good at. So before you reach your maximum potential training with a gym ball, the smart ones among you will be looking to introduce new challenges with different equipment like dumbbells, barbells, medicine balls or suspension training, as well as new challenges for cardiovascular fitness and flexibility.

As a personal trainer I know that I have a greater than average interest in the human body and the effects of exercise, partly because it is my passion and partly because it is my job. I also recognise that in the busy world we live in, expecting the same level of interest and dedication from clients towards health and exercise is unrealistic, so for me the best personal trainers are those who help clients to integrate exercise into everyday life rather than allow it to dominate.

The body is an amazing thing and responds to exercise by adapting and improving the way that it functions. Exercise is not all about pain, challenges and hard work, rather it is about making sure that in the long term your life includes the elements that have the greatest affect. I strongly believe that every minute you invest in exercise pays you back with interest, and that it's all about finding the right balance, which in a book about exercising with balls that improve balance is a good thought to end on. Finding that balance is different for all of us, but I think you can't go far wrong if you train for stability, strength and maybe power. Walk and run, eat healthily and drink water. Find time to relax and stretch, but above all remember: if you ever find yourself lacking in motivation, the best advice I can give anybody wanting to feel more healthy is that if you're moving, you're improving.

. . . .

fitness glossary

As a person interested in health and fitness there is no need to sound like you have swallowed a textbook for breakfast. Yes, you need to understand how things work, but I feel there is more skill in being able to explain complicated subjects in simple language rather than simply memorising a textbook. The following glossary sets out to explain the key words and phrases that, for a person interested in the body, are useful to know and will help you get the most out of this book, especially the training section.

Abdominals The name given to the group of muscles that make up the front of the torso, also known as 'the abs'.

Abduction The opposite of adduction (see below). The term the medical profession uses to describe any movement of a limb away from the midline of the body. So, if you raise your arm up to the side, that would be described as 'abduction of the shoulder'.

Acceleration The opposite of deceleration (see below). The speed at which a movement increases from start to finish. When using weights, accelerating the weight when moving it at a constant speed really adds to the challenge.

Adduction The opposite of abduction (see above). The term the medical profession uses to describe any movement of a limb across the midline of the body. So, if you cross your legs that would be 'adduction of the hip'.

Aerobic The opposite of anaerobic (see below). The word invented in 1968 by Dr Kenneth Cooper to describe the process in our body when we are working 'with oxygen'. While the term is now associated with the dance-based exercise to music (ETM), the original aerobic exercises that Cooper measured were cross country running, skiing, swimming, running, cycling and walking. Generally most people consider activity up to 80 per cent of maximum heart rate (MHR, see below) to be aerobic and beyond that to be anaerobic.

Age The effects of exercise change throughout life. With strength training in particular age will influence the outcome. As you reach approximately the age of 40, maintaining and developing lean muscle mass becomes harder and, in fact, the body starts to lose lean mass as a natural part of the ageing process. This can be combated somewhat with close attention to diet and exercise. At the other end of the scale a sensible approach is required when introducing very young people to training with weights.

Personally I don't like to see children participating in very heavy weight training, as it should not be pursued by boys and girls who are still growing (in terms of bone structure, rather than muscle structure), as excessive loading on prepubescent bones may have an adverse effect. There is very little conclusive research available on this subject, as it would require children to be put through tests that require them to lift very heavy weights in order to assess how much is too much. Newborn babies have over 300 bones and as we grow some bones fuse together leaving an adult with an average of 206 mature bones by age 20.

Agility Your progressive ability to move at speed and change direction while doing so.

Anaerobic The opposite of aerobic (see above). High intensity bursts of cardiovascular activity generally above 80 per cent of MHR. The term literally means 'without oxygen' because when operating at this speed, the body flicks over to the fuel stored in muscles rather than mixing the fuel first with oxygen, which is what happens during aerobic activity.

Anaerobic threshold The point at which the body cannot clear lactic acid fast enough to avoid a build-up in the bloodstream. The delaying of this occurrence is a major characteristic of performance athletes, their frequent high intensity training increases (delays) the point at which this waste product becomes overwhelming.

Assessment I like to say that if you don't assess, you guess, so before embarking on any exercise regime you should assess your health and fitness levels in a number of areas, which can include flexibility, range of motion, strength or any of the cardiac outputs that can be measured at home or in the laboratory.

Barbell A long bar (6–7ft) with disc weights loaded onto each end. Olympic bars are competition grade versions that rotate on bearings to enable very heavy weights to be lifted.

Biceps The muscle at the front of the arm. It makes up about one-third of the entire diameter of the upper arm with the triceps forming the other two-thirds.

Blood pressure When the heart contracts and squirts out blood the pressure on the walls of the blood vessels is the blood pressure. It is expressed as a fraction, for example 130/80. The 130 (systolic) is the high point of the pressure being exerted on the tubes and the 80 (diastolic) is the lower amount of pressure between the main pulses.

Body Pump This is a group exercise programme available in health clubs that changed the way people think about lifting weights simply by using music for timing and motivation. Rather than counting the reps, the class follow the set tunes and work around all the different muscle groups as the music tracks change.

Cardiovascular system (CV) This is the superhighway around the body. Heart, lungs and blood vessels transport and deliver the essentials of life: oxygen, energy, nutrients. Having delivered all this good stuff it then removes the rubbish by transporting away the waste products from the complex structure of muscle tissue.

Centre line This is an imaginary line that runs down the centre of the body from the chin to a point through the ribs, pelvis, right down to the floor.

Circuit A list of exercises can be described as a circuit. If you see '2 circuits' stated on a programme, it means you are expected to work through that list of exercises twice.

Concentric contraction The opposite of eccentric contraction (see below). If this word isn't familiar to you just think 'contract', as in to get smaller/shorter. A concentric contraction is when a muscle shortens under tension. For example, when you lift a cup towards your mouth you produce a concentric contraction of the bicep (don't make the mistake of thinking that when you lower the cup it's a concentric contraction of the opposite muscle, i.e. the triceps, as it isn't ... it's an eccentric movement of the bicep).

Contact points The parts of the body that are touching the bench, ball, wall or floor. The smaller the contact points, e.g. heels rather than entire foot, the greater the balance and stabilisation requirements of an exercise.

Core Ah, the core. Ask 10 trainers to describe the core and you will get 10 different answers. To me it is the obvious muscles of the abdominals, the lower back, etc., but it is also the smaller deep muscles and connective tissue that provide stability and strength to the individual. Muscles such as the glutes, hamstrings and, most importantly, the pelvic floor are often forgotten as playing a key role in the core. When I am doing a demonstration of core muscle activation, the way I sum up the core is that the majority of movements that require stability are in some way using all of the muscles that connect between the nipples and the knees.

Creatine An amino acid created naturally in your body. Every time you perform any intense exercise, e.g. weight training, your body uses creatine as a source of energy. The body has the ability to store more creatine than it produces, so taking it as a supplement would allow you to train for longer at high intensity. Consuming creatine is only productive when combined with high intensity training and, therefore, is not especially relevant until you start to train for power.

Cross training An excellent approach to fitness training where you use a variety of methods to improve your fitness rather than just one. Cross training is now used by athletes and sportspeople to reduce injury levels, as it ensures that you have a balanced amount of cardio, strength and flexibility in a schedule.

Deceleration The opposite of acceleration (see above). It is the decrease in velocity of an object. If you consider that injuries in sportspeople more often occur during the deceleration phase rather than the acceleration phase of their activity (for example, a sprinter pulling up at the end of the race rather than when they push out of the starting blocks), you will focus particularly on this phase of all the moves in this book. The power moves especially call for you to control the 'slowing down' part of the move, which requires as much skill as it does to generate the speed in the first place.

Delayed onset muscle soreness (DOMS) This is that unpleasant muscle soreness that you get after starting a new kind of activity or when you have worked harder than normal. It was once thought that the soreness was caused by lactic acid becoming 'trapped' in the muscle after a workout, but we now realise that this is simply not the case because lactic acid doesn't hang around – it is continuously moved and metabolised. The pain is far more likely to be caused by a mass of tiny little muscle tears. It's not a cure, but some light exercise will often ease the pain because this increases the flow of blood and nutrients to the damaged muscle tissue.

Deltoid A set of three muscles that sit on top of your shoulders.

. . . .

Dumbbell A weight designed to be lifted with one hand. It can be adjustable or of a fixed weight, and the range of weight available goes a rather pointless 1kg up to a massive 50kg plus.

Dynamometer A little gadget used to measure strength by squeezing a handheld device that then measures the force of your grip.

Dyna-Band® A strip of rubber used as an alternative to a dumbbell, often by physiotherapists for working muscles through specific ranges of motion where weights are either too intense or can't target the appropriate muscles. Dyna-Band® can be held flat against the skin to give subtle muscle stimulation, for example, by wrapping a strip around the shoulders (like an Egyptian mummy), you can then work through protraction and retraction movements of the shoulder girdle.

Eccentric contraction The opposite of concentric contraction (see above). The technical term for when a muscle is lengthening under tension. An easy example to remember is the lowering of a dumbbell during a bicep curl, which is described as an eccentric contraction of the bicep.

Eye line Where you are looking when performing movements. Some movement pattens are significantly altered by correct or incorrect eye line, for example, if the eye line is too high during squats, then the head is lifted and the spine will experience excessive extension.

Fascia Connective tissue that attaches muscles to muscles and enables individual muscle fibres to be bundled together. While not particularly scientific, a good way to visualise fascia is that it performs in a similar way to the skin of a sausage by keeping its contents where it should be.

Fitball (gym ball, stability ball, Swiss ball) The large balls extensively used for stability training by therapists and in gyms. They are available in sizes 55–75cm. If you are using them for weight training always remember to add your weight and the dumbbell weight together to make sure the total weight doesn't exceed the safety limit of the ball.

Flexibility The misconception is that we do flexibility to actually stretch the muscle fibres and make them longer, whereas, in fact, when we stretch effectively it is the individual muscle fibres that end up moving more freely against each other, creating a freer increased range of motion.

Foam rolling This is a therapy technique that has become mainstream. You use a round length of foam to massage your own muscles (generally you sit or lie on the roller to exert force via your body weight). Interestingly, while this has a positive effect on your muscle fibres, it is the fascia that is 'stretched' most. Foam rolling is actually rather painful when you begin, but as you improve, the pain decreases. Often used by athletes as part of their warm-up.

Free weights The collective name for dumbbells and barbells. There has been a huge influx of new products entering this category so in the free weights area of a good gym you will also find kettlebells and medicine balls. In bodybuilding gyms you will often find items not designed for exercise but which are challenging to lift and use, such as heavy chains, ropes and tractor tyres.

Functional training Really all training should be functional as it is the pursuit of methods and movements that benefit you in day to day life. Therefore, doing squats are functionally beneficial for your abdominals because they work them in conjunction with other muscles, but sit-ups are not because they don't work the abdominals in a way that relates to many everyday movements.

Gait Usually associated with running and used to describe the way that a runner hits the ground either with the inside, centre or outside of their foot and, specifically, how the foot, ankle and knee joints move. However, this term always relates to how you stand and walk. Mechanical issues that exist below the knee can have a knock-on effect on other joints and muscles throughout the body. Pronation is the name given to the natural inward roll of the ankle that occurs when the heel strikes the ground and the foot flattens out. Supination refers to the opposite outward roll that occurs during the push-off phase of the walking and running movement. A mild amount of pronation and supination is both healthy and necessary to propel the body forward.

Genes As in the hereditary blueprint that you inherited from your parents, rather than the blue denim variety. Genes can influence everything from your hair colour to your predisposition to developing diseases. Clearly there is nothing you can do to influence your genes, so accept that some athletes are born great because they have the odds stacked on their side while others have to train their way to glory.

Gluteus maximus A set of muscles on your bottom, also known as 'the glutes'.

Hamstring A big set of muscles down the back of the thigh. It plays a key role in core stability and needs to be flexible if you are to develop a good squat technique.

Heart rate (HR) Also called 'the pulse'. It is the number of times each minute that your heart contracts. An athlete's HR could be as low as 35 beats per minute (BPM) when resting but can also go up to 250BPM during activity.

Hypertrophy The growth of skeletal muscle. This is what a bodybuilder is constantly trying to do. The number of muscle fibres we have is fixed, so rather than 'growing' new muscles fibres hypertrophy is the process of increasing the size of the existing fibre. Building muscle is a slow and complex process that requires constant training and a detailed approach to nutrition.

Insertion All muscles are attached to bone or other muscles by tendons or fascia. The end of the muscle that moves during a contraction is the insertion, with the moving end being called the origin. Note that some muscles have more than one origin and insertion.

Integration (compound) The opposite of isolation (see below). Movement that requires more than one joint and muscle to be involved, e.g. a squat.

Isolation The opposite of integration (see above). A movement that requires only one joint and muscle to be involved, e.g. a bicep curl.

Interval training A type of training where you do blocks of high intensity exercise followed by a block of lower intensity (recovery) exercise. The blocks can be time based or marked by distance (in cardio training). Interval training is highly beneficial to both athletes and fitness enthusiasts as it allows them to subject their body to high intensity activity in short achievable bursts.

Intra-abdominal pressure (IAP) An internal force that assists in the stabilisation of the lumber spine. This relates to the collective effects of pressure exerted on the structures of the diaphragm, transversus abdominis, multifidi and the pelvic floor.

Kinesiology The scientific study of the movement of our anatomical structure. It was only in the 1960s with the creation of fixed weight machines that we started to isolate individual muscles and work them one at a time. This is a step backwards in terms of kinesiology because in real life a single muscle rarely works in isolation.

Kinetic chain The series of reactions/forces throughout the nerves, bones, muscles, ligaments and tendons when the body moves or has a force applied against it.

Kyphosis Excessive curvature of the human spine. This can range from being a little bit round shouldered to being in need of corrective surgery.

Lactic acid A by-product of muscle contractions. If lactic acid reaches a level higher than that which the body can quickly clear from the blood stream, the person has reached their anaerobic threshold. Training at high intensity has the effect of delaying the point at which lactic acid levels cause fatigue.

Latissimus dorsi Two triangular-shaped muscles that run from the top of the neck and spine to the back of the upper arm and all the way into the lower back, also known as 'the lats'.

Ligaments Connective tissues that attach bone to bone or cartilage to bone. They have fewer blood vessels passing through them than muscles, which makes them whiter (they look like gristle) and also slower to heal.

Lordosis Excessive curvature of the lower spine. Mild cases that are diagnosed early can often be resolved through core training and by working on flexibility with exercises best prescribed by a physiotherapist.

Massage Not just for pleasure or relaxation, this can speed up recovery and reduce discomfort after a hard training session. Massage can help maintain range of motion in joints and reduce mild swelling caused by injury related inflammation.

Magnesium An essential mineral that plays a role in over 300 processes in the body including in the cardiovascular system and tissue repair.

Maximum heart rate (MHR) The highest number of times the heart can contract (or beat) in one minute. A very approximate figure can be obtained for adults by using the following formula: 220 – current age = MHR. Athletes often exceed this guideline, but only because they have progressively pushed themselves and increased their strength over time.

Medicine ball Traditionally this was a leather ball packed with fibre to make it heavy. Modern versions are solid rubber or filled with a heavy gel.

Mobility The ability of a joint to move freely through a range of motion. Mobility is very important because if you have restricted joint mobility and with exercise you start to load that area with weights, the chances are that you will compound the problem.

Muscular endurance (MSE) The combination of strength and endurance. The ability to perform many repetitions against a given resistance for a prolonged period. In strength training any more than 12 reps is considered MSE.

Negative-resistance training (NRT) Resistance training in which the muscles lengthen while still under tension. Lowering a barbell, bending down and running downhill are all examples. It is felt that this type of training will increase muscle size more quickly than other types of training, but if you only ever do NRT you won't be training the body to develop usable functional strength.

Obliques The muscles on both sides of the abdomen that rotate and flex the torso. Working these will have no effect on 'love handles', which are fat that sits above, but is not connected to, the obliques.

Origin All muscles are attached to bone or others muscles by tendons or fascia. The end of the muscle which is not moved during a contraction is the origin, with the moving end being called the insertion. Note that some muscles have more than one origin and insertion.

Overtraining Excessive amounts of exercise, intensity, or both volume and intensity of training, resulting in fatigue, illness, injury and/or impaired performance. Overtraining can occur in individual parts of the body or throughout, which is a good reason for keeping records of the training you do so you can see if patterns of injuries relate to a certain time or types of training you do throughout the year.

Patience With strength training – more than any other type of exercise – patience is essential. When you exercise the results are based on the ability of the body to 'change', which includes changes in the nervous system as well as progressive improvements in the soft tissues (muscles, ligaments and tendons). While it is not instantly obvious why patience is so important, it becomes clearer when you consider how, for example, the speed of change differs in the blood rich muscles at a faster rate than the more avascular ligaments and tendons. Improvements take time so be patient.

Pectorals The muscles of the chest, also known as 'the pecs'. Working the pecs will have a positive effect on the appearance of the chest, however, despite claims, it is unlikely that working the pecs will have any effect on the size of female breasts although it can make them feel firmer if the muscle tone beneath them is increased.

Pelvic floor (PF) Five layers of muscle and connective tissue at the base of the torso. The male and female anatomy differs in this area, however strength and endurance is essential in the PF for both men and women if you are to attain maximum strength in the core. Most of the core training or stability products work the PF.

Periodisation Sums up the difference between a long-term strategy and short-term gains. Periodisation is where you plan to train the body for different outcomes throughout a year or longer. The simplest version of this method would be where a track athlete worked on muscle strength and growth during the winter and then speed and maintenance of muscle endurance during the summer racing session.

Planes of motion The body moves through three planes of motion. Sagittal describes all the forward and back movement; frontal describes the side to side movements; and transverse describes the rotational movements. In everyday life most of the movements we go through involve actions from all three planes all of the time –it is really only 'artificial' techniques, such as bicep curls and deltoid raises, that call upon just one plane at a time.

Plyometrics An explosive movement practised by athletes, for example, two-footed jumps over hurdles. This is not for beginners or those with poor levels of flexibility and/or a limited range of motion.

Prone Lying face down, also the standard description of exercises performed from a lying face down position. The opposite of supine (see below).

Protein A vital nutrient that needs to be consumed every day. Carbohydrates provide your body with energy, while protein helps your muscles to recover and repair more quickly after exercise. Foods high in protein include whey protein, which is a by-product of the dairy industry and is consumed as a shake, fish, chicken, eggs, dairy produce (such as milk, cheese and yoghurt), beef and soya.

Increased activity will increase your protein requirements. A lack of quality protein can result in loss of muscle tissue and tone, a weaker immune system, slower recovery and lack of energy. The protein supplements industry has developed many convenient methods for consuming protein in the form of powders, shakes and food bars, most of which contain the most easily digested and absorbable type of protein, whey protein.

Pyramid A programming method for experienced weight trainers. A set of the same exercises are performed at least three times, each set has progressively fewer repetitions in it, but greater resistance. When you reach the peak of the pyramid (heaviest weight) you then perform the same three sets again in reverse order. For example, going up the pyramid would ask for 15 reps with 10kg, 10 reps with 15kg, 5 reps with 20kg. Going down the pyramid would require 10 reps with 15kg, 15 reps with 10kg.

Quadriceps The groups of muscles at the front of the thighs, also known as 'the quads'. They are usually the first four muscle names that personal trainers learn, but in case you have forgotten the four are: vastus intermedius, rectus femoris (that's the one that's also a hip flexor), vastus lateralis and vastus medialis.

Range of motion (ROM) The degree of movement that occurs at one of the body's joints. Without physio equipment it is difficult to measure a joint precisely, however, you can easily compare the shoulder, spine, hip, knee and ankle on the left side with the range of motion of the same joints on the right side.

Reebok Core Board® A stability product that you predominately stand on. The platform has a central axis which creates a similar experience to using a wobble board, however the Reebok Core Board® also rotates under tension so you can train against torsion and recoil.

Recoil The elastic characteristic of muscle when 'stretched' to return the body parts back to the start positions after a dynamic movement.

Recovery/rest The period when not exercising and the most important component of any exercise programme. It is only during rest periods that the body adapts to previous training loads and rebuilds itself to be stronger, thereby facilitating improvement. Rest is therefore vitally important for progression.

Repetitions How many of each movement you do, also known as 'reps'. On training programmes you will have see three numerical figures that you need to understand – reps, sets and circuits.

Repetition max (RM) The maximum load that a muscle or muscle group can lift. Establishing your 1RM can help you select the right amount of weight for different exercises and it is also a good way of monitoring progress.

Resistance training Any type of training with weights, including gym machines, barbells and dumbbells and bodyweight exercises.

Resting heart rate (RHR) The number of contractions (heartbeats) per minute when at rest. The average RHR for an adult is approx 72BPM, but for athletes it can be much lower.

Scapula retraction Not literally 'pulling your shoulders back', but that is a good cue to use to get this desired effect. Many people develop rounded shoulders, which when lifting weights puts them at a disadvantage because the scapular cannot move freely, so by lifting the ribs and squeezing the shoulder blades back the shoulder girdle is placed in a good lifting start position.

Sciatica Layman's term for back pain which radiates through the spine, buttocks and hamstrings. Usually due to pressure on the sciatic nerve being shortened, which runs from the lower back and down the legs, rather than being a problem with the skeleton. Most often present in people who sit a lot. Core training, massage and flexibility exercises can frequently cure the problem.

Set A block of exercises usually put together to work an area of the body to the point of fatigue, so if you were working legs you may do squats, lunges and calf raises straight after each other, then repeat them again for a second 'set'.

Speed, agility and quickness (SAQ)® Although in fact a brand name, this has become the term used to describe a style of exercises or drills which are designed to improve speed, agility and quickness. Very athletic and dynamic, often including plyometric movements.

Stability ball (also gym ball, fitball and Swiss ball) The large balls extensively used for suitability training by therapists and in gyms. They are available in sizes 55–75cm. If you are using them for weight training always remember to add your weight and the dumbbell weight together to make sure the total weight doesn't exceed the safety limit of the ball.

Stretch A balanced approach to stretching is one of the most important elements of feeling good and reducing the likelihood of developing non-trauma soft tissue injuries. When we lift weight clearly the muscle fatigues and as a result at the end of the session the overall muscle (rather than individual fibres) can feel 'tight' or shortened. Doing a stretch will help return the muscle to its pre-exercise state. Dynamic stretching (rhythmic movements to promote optimum range of movement from muscle/joints) should be performed pre-workout. Static stretching performed after the gym ball session is productive as long as you dedicate enough time to each position, so give each section of the body worked at least 90 seconds of attention.

Suspension training A strength training format that allows you to use your body weight as the resistance by means of hanging from long adjustable straps that are suspended above head height, also known as 'TRX®'. By adjusting the length of the straps and changing the body and foot position the challenge can be adapted for all levels of ability.

Superset Similar to a set, but each sequential exercise is performed with no rest in between. The moves in a superset are selected to ensure that they relate to each other, for example, an exercise that focused on shoulders and triceps, such as a shoulder press, would be followed by another shoulder/triceps move, such as dips.

Supine Lying face up, also the standard description of exercises performed from a lying face up position. The opposite of prone (see above).

Tendon Connective tissue that attaches muscles to bones. Muscle and tendon tissue merge together progressively, rather than there being a clear line where tendon starts and muscle finishes. Like ligaments, a tendon has fewer blood vessels running through it and is less flexible than muscle tissue.

Time As a personal trainer, I have been asked many times, 'What is the best time of day to exercise?' The answer depends. If you are an athlete training almost every day perhaps twice a day, then I would say that strength training in the morning could be more productive than at other times due to the body clock and fluctuating hormone levels throughout the day. However, if the question is asked by a casual exerciser with an average diet and a job and busy lifestyle, my answer would be to exercise at any time of the day, as exercise is a productive use of your valuable free time.

Torsion Stress on the body when external forces twist it about the spinal axis.

Training partner A training partner can be a person who keeps you company and motivates you while you exercise or they can also take the role of being your 'spotter' when you are lifting heavy weights. The role of a spotter is to hand and take the weights from you when you are fatigued from a heavy set of lifts. Choose your partner wisely; weights can be dangerous, so ensure they take the responsibility seriously.

Training shoes The best shoes to wear when lifting weights will have a combination of good grip and stability. Some athletes are now choosing to lift while wearing no or very thin soled shoes on the basis that it will work the muscles in their feet more and therefore give greater results – if you do consider doing this take a number of weeks to build up the amount you do barefoot to give the feet time to strengthen slowly. Athletes competing in powerlifting contests will wear performance shoes that give their feet increased support, however these are not suitable for exercises in which the foot is moved.

Transversus abdominis A relatively thin sheet of muscle which wraps around the torso. This is the muscle that many people think they activate by following the instruction of 'pull your stomach in', however that movement is more likely to be facilitated by the main abdominals. For your information, a flat stomach is more likely to be achieved by simply standing up straight, as this ensures the correct distance between the ribs and pelvis.

Triceps Muscles at the back of the upper arms. They make up approximately two-thirds of the diameter of the upper arm, so if arm size is your goal, working the triceps will be a priority.

Vertebrae Individual bones that make up the spinal column. The intervertebral discs that sit between them are there to keep the vertebrae separated, cushion the spine and protect the spinal cord.

VO$_2$ max The highest volume of oxygen a person can infuse into their blood during exercise. A variety of calculations or tests can be used to establish your VO$_2$ max; these include measuring the heart rate during and post aerobic activity. As each of these tests includes a measurement of the distance covered as well as the heart's reaction to activity, the most popular methods of testing VO$_2$ max are running, stepping, swimming or cycling for a set time and distance.

Warm-up The first part of any workout session that is intended to prepare the body for the exercise ahead of it. I find it is best to take the lead from the sports world and base the warm-up exactly on the movements you will do in the session. So if you are about to do weights rather than jog, go through some of the movements unloaded to prepare the body for the ranges of motion you will later be doing loaded.

Warm-down The slowing down or controlled recovery period after a workout session. A warm-down can include low level cardio work to return the heart rate to a normal speed as well as stretching and relaxation.

Wobble board A circular wooden disc that you stand on with a hemisphere on one side. Originally used just by physiotherapists, they are now common in gyms and are used for stability training, core exercises and strengthening the ankle and/or rehabilitation from ankle injuries. Technology has been applied to this simple piece of equipment and you now have progressive devices such as the Reebok Core Board® and the BOSU® (Both sides up), which achieve the same and more than the wooden versions.

X-training, activity. See cross training (above).

Yoga Probably the oldest form of fitness training in existence. Yoga has many different types (or styles) ranging from very passive stretching techniques through to explosive and dynamic style. It is often associated with hippy culture and 'yummy mummies', however, if you are doing any type of strength training, yoga will compliment this nicely.

about the author

STEVE BARRETT is a former national competitor in athletics, rugby, mountain biking and sport aerobics. His career in the fitness industry as a personal trainer spans over 20 years. His work as a lecturer and presenter has taken him to 32 countries including the United States, Russia and Australia.

For many years Steve delivered Reebok International's fitness strategy and implementation via their training faculty Reebok University. He gained the title of Reebok Global Master Trainer, which is a certification that required a minimum of three years' studying, presenting and researching both practical and academic subjects. Between the years 2000 and 2008 in this role he lectured and presented to more than 20,000 fellow fitness professionals and students.

Steve played a key role in the development of the training systems and launch of two significant products in the fitness industry: the Reebok Deck and Reebok Core Board®. As a personal trainer, in addition to teaching the teachers and working with the rich and famous he has been involved in the training of many international athletes and sports personalities at Liverpool FC, Arsenal FC, Manchester Utd FC, the Welsh RFU, and UK athletics.

Within the fitness industry he has acted as a consultant to leading brand names, including Nestlé, Kelloggs, Reebok and Adidas.

His media experience includes being guest expert for the BBC and writing for numerous publications including *The Times*, *The Independent*, *The Daily Telegraph*, *Runner's World*, *Men's Fitness*, *Rugby News*, *Health & Fitness*, *Zest*, *Ultra-FIT*, *Men's Health UK* and *Australia* and many more.

Steve's expertise is in the development of logical, user friendly, safe and effective training programmes. The work that he is most proud of, however, isn't his celebrity projects, but the changes to ordinary people's lives that never get reported.

Now that he has been teaching fitness throughout his 20s, 30s and now 40s, he has developed a tremendous ability to relate to the challenges that people face to incorporate exercise into their lifestyle, and while the fitness industry expects personal trainers to work with clients for a short period of time, Steve has been working with many of his clients for nearly two decades, continuously evolving to meet their changing needs.

His fun and direct approach has resulted in many couch potatoes running out of excuses and transforming into fitness converts.

www.Trade-Secrets-of-a-Personal-Trainer.com

index